HUMANE POLICING

HOW PERSPECTIVES CAN INFLUENCE OUR PERFORMANCE

By Darron Spencer

Inspire On Purpose Publishing
Irving, Texas

Humane Policing: How Perspectives Can Influence Our Performance

Inspire On Purpose Publishing
Irving, Texas
(888) 403-2727
https://inspireonpurpose.com
The Platform Publisher™

Printed in the United States of America

Library of Congress Control Number: 2017933511

ISBN-10: 1-941782-42-6

ISBN-13: 978-1-941782-42-2

NOTE TO READERS

While identifying names, details, and case numbers have all been removed from the stories highlighted in *Humane Policing: How Perspectives Can Influence Our Performance*, I would like readers to consider the reports police officers write as more than mere documents establishing fact. They are in fact a prelude to the war – i.e., the legal battle – that is about to begin. The officer and suspect are not combatants in the war but rather are spectators, and both can quickly become causalities if they are not diligent.

The prosecutor and defense attorney wage the war by making logical arguments against each other's side. The officer provides ammunition and areas of advancement for the prosecutor. If corners are cut, if information is omitted, or if the areas of advancement are not properly established, the defense attorney will destroy the officer and win the war.

Likewise, if suspects are not diligent in their selection of a defense attorney, flaws in the prosecutor's battle plans can be missed, causing suspects to become causalities, requiring them to fight another day or serve the time determined after losing the war.

The best war is the war that's never fought.

Michelle Morse

Rebecca Chown

TABLE OF CONTENTS

INTRODUCTION

My Vow to Protect and Serve

When you put on a uniform,
there are certain inhibitions that you accept.

DWIGHT D. EISENHOWER

My journey into law enforcement began five years ago. A former Marine infantryman, I was excited to begin a new chapter in my life that my wife would be proud of, that would allow my son to embrace a new hero, and that would allow me to assume the role of protecting my community with immense pride, hope, and commitment.

On April 16, 2012, I joined a sheriff's office with a jurisdiction spanning more than 4,000 square miles. This vast county included seven cities, 23 towns, and acre upon acre of sprawling plains. For my first nine months, I worked as a corrections officer in an island of brick and mortar otherwise known as North Jail Complex containing approximately 600 offenders.

Between my training time at the jail's in-house academy, my work as a corrections officer, my time recovering from an on-the-job injury, my time at the patrol officer's in-house academy, my field training, and my time as a patrol deputy, I was with the sheriff's office for three years.

In most sheriffs' offices, people transition from working as corrections officers at jails to becoming patrol deputies who more or less have the same duties as police officers but with larger jurisdictions and slightly different requirements statutorily.

Corrections officers enforce the rules and regulations of the facility in which they work, while patrol deputies and police officers enforce laws and have the power to charge people with crimes and arrest them. The difference between patrol deputies and police officers is that patrol deputies have jurisdiction over the entire county, while the jurisdiction of police officers is limited to the city they work in.

When I joined the sheriff's office, I was handed an official uniform to distinguish me for the services I was fully prepared to perform. With that uniform, I donned the uncertainty each day would bring along with a spectrum of emotions I would come to know intimately ranging from elation to sadness to rage.

In my 20 months in the patrol division before an unexpected physical disability forced me to step down, I was recognized as Deputy of the Year and received the Ribbon of Merit. My more than 250 cases resulted in 40 felony and 74 misdemeanor arrests, and I personally wrote 57 warrantless arrest affidavits, seven arrest warrants, two production of records, and a single search warrant. I also assisted in four death investigations and booked over 150 items of evidence. My cases were forwarded to the military, the Federal Bureau of Investigation, the Department of Alcohol, Tobacco, and Firearms, the Gang Task Force, U.S. Immigration and Customs Enforcement, the Drug Task Force, and numerous local agencies.

If it appears I covered an enormous number of cases in a short amount of time, it's because I did. I can't explain why, but I always seemed to be on duty when the calls came in. A few key cases I worked on included:

- Coordinating, tracking, and arresting an attempted homicide suspect
- Investigating a stolen handgun exchange at a high school
- Investigating and forwarding the first confirmed state-wide case of the flesh-eating opioid drug known as krocodil
- Investigating and forwarding a case involving a defaced assault rifle and potential gun supplier to members of the Hell's Angels motorcycle gang

- Processing and investigating a theft from a military installation linked to several bases, whereupon the subsequent arrests solved five crimes simultaneously

- Submitting two separate work-ups to crime analysis for people and vehicles involved with methamphetamines

The statistic I'm most proud of is that 90% of the individuals I arrested thanked me.

Let me emphasize that: 90% of the individuals I arrested *thanked* me. Why? How? I arrested these people; what did I do to earn their thanks?

Explaining my approach to law enforcement and how I worked to change perspectives, improve relationships, and induce cooperation rather than force compliance is the topic of this book. Of necessity, a twin purpose in writing this book is to address the crisis in our society involving the all-too-frequently inhumane and unproductive – even when lawful – interactions between law enforcement and the people we vow to serve and protect.

Because of the rapport I was able to build with those I came into contact with, I have valuable information to share that could benefit every individual in the United States of America while creating more harmony in the name of justice.

I wrote this book for my fellow law enforcement professionals but also for the general public. If you are a member of the law enforcement community, I hope you'll appreciate the success I achieved by implementing a deliberate and consistent manner of engagement with the general public. In addition, I hope you'll consider adopting this approach yourself. Not only will it garner you the respect of the people you serve, but it will also make your duties far easier and safer for everyone concerned.

If you are not pursuing a career in law enforcement, I hope to educate and enlighten you about the complexities of the job so you'll better understand why our men and women in uniform take the actions they do. Examples of actual cases will shed light on the types of appropriate (and at times inappropriate) actions you can expect from law enforcement, and I hope you will feel compelled to respond in kind.

Using a variety of actual cases, *Humane Policing* takes a closer look at how those enforcing the law and those suspected of breaking it might alter how they interact. The benefit of building a more positive relationship between various law enforcement entities and the general public could affect positive changes on both sides of the divide while saving precious lives.

While such a transformation will take time, once a clear change in philosophy is routinely demonstrated, the general public might become more inclined to praise and honor our officers for the service they provide than for their willingness to make the ultimate sacrifice.

After the terrorist attacks of 9/11, it became routine to honor and hold in high esteem members of the military for their commitment and service, both past and present. I believe we should do no less for the "soldiers of law enforcement" who work and risk their lives on the streets of our great nation. To achieve this new level of respect, the peacekeepers of our country must learn and mindfully practice a new way of interacting with the public.

Similar to those who came before me, I swore an oath to protect and serve my community and the community at large. For the purpose of telling the stories contained in *Humane Policing: How Perspectives Can Influence Our Performance*, I extend a similar oath to you, and with the same level of commitment, to tell the truth, the whole truth, and nothing but the truth, to the very best of my ability.

Why Law Enforcement Needs to Change

We cannot change unless we survive,
but we will not survive unless we change.

UNKNOWN

Our society and culture have a widespread and deeply rooted problem. Namely, a great divide exists between the law enforcement officers who protect our city streets and county roads and the citizens who traverse them. Alas, that divide seems to grow wider by the day.

This apparent disconnect between law enforcement and the general public is complicated. Analyzing it is not the goal of this book. Suffice it to say that the problem is rooted in the fact that the public doesn't understand what we do or why we do it. Law enforcement officers are needed – everyone knows this and willingly admits it – but people fear us and feel like we're out to get them.

The fact is, we're out to help people, and I know for a fact that in my 20 months as a patrol deputy, I succeeded. It's why over 90% of those I arrested thanked me. Upon receiving such thanks, I often replied, "I pride myself on my customer service." Inevitably, this made people chuckle. It was a crazy thing to say, but I meant it.

Sometimes it quite literally takes an act of God in the form of an earthquake, flooding, hurricanes, or some other natural disaster for people to fully respect law enforcement officers. Without question, everyone appreciates our humanitarian side. It's the other sides that leave something more to be desired.

For now, let's briefly imagine a better scenario. What if we law enforcement officers were able to neutralize the negativity that permeates this great divide and even turn it into a positive? Such a change would improve relationships, preserve lives, and allow our great men and women in uniform to enjoy long and fulfilling careers.

Let's review a few facts related to law enforcement that are undeniable yet not often discussed. Many of our great men and women in uniform who have answered the call to protect and serve the public suffer adverse effects from working in a constantly negative atmosphere and dealing with skewed public perceptions. For example, over one hundred law enforcement personnel take their own lives every year. These preventable deaths more than double the number of officers killed in the line of duty in felonious incidents each year.

Of those law enforcement officers who don't take their own lives, many become cynical, further alienating the general public. In part, this is because law enforcement officers are primarily trained to look for and address the negative aspects of people's lives. This constant focus on negative circumstances often causes us to develop a cynical outlook on people in general. This is why I believe it is so important for the general public to acknowledge and appreciate the level of commitment and sacrifice law enforcement officers make while faithfully serving our communities.

I am not making excuses or justifying questionable actions taken by relatively few among us. Like any profession, some people in our ranks should not be allowed to serve in any law enforcement capacity. It is a unique profession, but the vast majority who choose this career feel a great desire to serve their communities. To me, that is a goal worthy of respect. It's true that upholding the law can be a thankless profession, but this was never a problem for me.

For one thing, I expected people to be unhappy to see me and to behave accordingly, so it never threw me or made me angry or impatient when they did. At worst, they met my expectations. At best, I was pleasantly surprised. Furthermore, the manner in which I approached people was usually met with positive results, so my behavior was positively reinforced.

Meanwhile, of those who proudly answer the call, not nearly enough actually retire from the profession. Part of the current crisis is that good law enforcement officers are leaving the profession, having determined that the current environment provides substantial risks and little reward. At the same time, in stark contrast to the situation back in 2004, when hundreds of applicants applied for every available law enforcement position, it's hard to find qualified people to fill open positions today.

Obvious benefits to law enforcement personnel of a transformed relationship between themselves and the public include an improvement in their general health, a decrease in the burnout rate, more patient and consequently more effective interactions with the public, and a better outlook that benefits careers and personal lives alike. Not only will this new and better approach enable law enforcement to get more out of their profession, but it will also eliminate a great deal of the cynicism and negative perception the general public feels towards law enforcement.

Inevitably, the risk of harm substantially increases whenever police officers or individuals in the public take a combative stance. Such situations cannot always be prevented, but when safety isn't an imminent concern, my experiences suggest that law enforcement officers must rethink the philosophy of "Ask them. Tell them. Make them." In short, we must stop policing through intimidation and replace this approach with genuine concern and patience for those suspected of wrongdoing.

Consider the possibilities if law enforcement personnel, instead of walking into a situation prepared to ask them, tell them, and make them, first considered an approach that relies on the following basic ideas instead:

- Addressing the initial perception and reactions of the individuals involved *before* acting
- Remaining calm when being tested
- Receiving and redirecting resentment for law enforcement
- Starting a conversation to get individuals talking
- Listening for key factors to improve rapport
- Having individuals give you leads and help you track people down
- Gaining cooperation by giving individuals a moral victory and allowing them to salvage some pride

- Maintaining patience and professionalism to change the perspective of individuals and bystanders alike

- Rewarding positive behavior from both individuals and bystanders

In my experience, an approach that encompasses these ideas opens dialogue and produces useful results with people suspected of wrongdoing. Quite often, the information gleaned from these conversations provides clues to ongoing cases or paves the way to effective solutions in which no one gets hurt.

Despite the apparent dangers, the majority of law enforcement officers sign up for the job because they want to help people. With that goal in mind, let's start paying attention to the nuances that are a large part of the job while working harder to stop coming across as bullies. No one likes a bully, it isn't necessary to be a bully, and playing the part of a bully often leads to the tragic but avoidable situation called officer-induced jeopardy.

Officer-Induced Jeopardy Is a Real Problem

Human progress is neither automatic nor inevitable...
Every step toward the goal of justice requires sacrifice,
suffering, and struggle; the tireless exertions and passionate
concern of dedicated individuals.

MARTIN LUTHER KING JR.

Officer-induced jeopardy occurs when a police officer has the option to take a different approach to achieve the desired results but instead forces a situation, with an unnecessarily negative outcome.

Fortunately, with proper training and a solid understanding of the importance of self-control, officers can avoid such situations. The following example reveals how a dual understanding of the law and my own nature allowed me to avoid escalating a situation and causing additional problems for everyone, myself included.

In this particular case, a woman called to ask us to check on her mother's well-being. The mother was supposedly meeting the caller's brother at the mother's residence, and the worried caller said her brother was a drug user. She gave me his date of birth, and I soon discovered that his driver's license was revoked but that he didn't have any active warrants.

When I arrived, the front door of the residence was open, but the glass storm door was shut. While walking up the driveway, I felt the exhaust pipe of the vehicle in the driveway. It was still hot, indicating it had been driven recently, so I recorded the vehicle and plate information.

Through the door, I spoke with a very edgy and aggressive male who didn't identify himself but who answered to the first name of the brother. It was hard to hear him through the door, so I told him I was going to open it, but I'm not sure he heard or understood me.

When I opened the door and held it open against my back, the male raised his voice and became increasingly aggressive. This was cause for concern because I could see various tools on the floor about five feet away, including a hatchet.

I calmly explained that I had been asked to check on the well-being of the residents. The male stated that he was fine, but his eyes were red and bloodshot and he never stopped pacing or waving his arms.

I asked who else lived at the address, and the man didn't respond. I asked again, and he mentioned a name I didn't understand or recognize. Since his behavior was odd and aggressive and his actions suggested he was under the influence of drugs, I requested a second unit as backup and for medical to stand by.

I asked the man where his mother was, and he stated that he didn't know. He said he didn't touch her or talk to her. I asked if she was still located at the residence, and he said no. I asked if he knew where she was, and he yelled, "No! I told you I didn't talk to her!"

When backup arrived and another officer began talking with the male, I retreated to my vehicle and called dispatch to request the cell phone number of the mother. After reaching her, I confirmed that she was not at the residence in question and that she was fine.

While in my cruiser, I heard an officer yell, "Don't pick up the hatchet!"

It was clear the subject was increasingly agitated by our presence, so I took the opportunity to diffuse the situation and approach it from a different angle.

I returned to the house and asked the male if he would talk to medical. He said no. I told him I'd reached his mother and that she was fine, and he thanked me. Since the well-being of the mother was no longer a concern, I cancelled medical and left the scene. We'd been contacted to check on the mother's well-being, and we'd done that successfully.

I could have articulated a medical hold for the individual, but I had limited legal grounds, given that he was on private property. Since officers who escalate a situation unnecessarily can be held liable for any negative out-comes, my best bet was to implement a better plan that initiated contact with the man elsewhere.

It was apparent he had arrived at and intended to leave the premises in a motor vehicle. Since I suspected he was under the influence of drugs and I knew his driver's license was revoked, seeing him behind the wheel would give me legal reason to stop and arrest him.

To that end, I parked at the exit of the neighborhood and waited for the man to drive away. Unfortunately, before I could catch him departing the neighborhood, I received a call in progress that required my immediate attention.

Had I forced the situation at the residence, there was a very good chance the subject would have attempted to attack me or one of the other officers on the scene with the hatchet. In such an instance, the likelihood of him being shot surely would have increased, and I could have been held liable for creating the situation.

Self-control on my part and a clear understanding of my duties and obligations allowed me to avoid escalating a situation that could have quickly become tragic. Nonetheless, that's sometimes easier said than done, as the following chapters indicate.

Shaping My Perspective

A moment's insight is sometimes worth a life's experience.

OLIVER WENDELL HOLMES

My work schedule at the jail during my nine months as a corrections officer was four days on and four days off, with a one-hour lunch break over a 13-hour shift. I alternated between the day and night shifts every six weeks.

It wasn't easy to go from days to nights, and I found this constant switch in scheduling tough to implement and sustain. Nonetheless, my time at the jail helped permanently shape my perspective toward inmates and my views on how best to treat them as well as any other individuals I investigated or arrested.

A unit at the jail consisted of 20 to 60 inmates. The higher their classification, the lower the number of inmates. In a traditional facility, inmates are viewed by cameras or through physical barriers like bars or windows. In my opinion, this type of environment allows the inmates to control and manipulate the unit by hiding and operating behind those barriers. In so doing, it creates a more dangerous environment for everyone.

Happily, the sheriff's office in my county managed inmates through a system referred to as direct supervision. This system places officers inside the units with the inmates. Being in the unit gives officers firsthand information, allows us to gain a better perspective of current activity, removes the physical barriers between us and the inmates, and reduces the level of inmate resentment. Not only is it a safer way to manage inmates, but it's also more humane because it allows us to get to know individual offenders as people rather than as criminals.

In addition, getting to know inmates on a more personal level is also extremely beneficial when it comes to investigating ancillary crimes inside and outside the facility. More specifically, direct supervision highlights the connections between groups and gang members within the jail population. Recognizing those connections enables us to assist our fellow officers outside of the facility to follow up on leads of criminal activity being initiated from the criminals in our custody. Whether inmates are attempting to contact known associates via phone or mail, possibly to violate a protection order, intimidate a witness, or plan a crime, we can gather intelligence and go from there.

My duties involved recording and supervising many activities, including handing out food trays. There were usually a few extra trays on the cart, and we corrections officers were encouraged to take a tray and eat with the inmates. They would sit at their tables while we ate at our desks some distance away, but we still had the sense of sharing a meal together. There were no bars or windows between us; we were in the same room. For a lot of people, it would be a scary proposition to be locked in a room with 60 inmates, but that's exactly the situation we were in. I was amazed at how effective it was.

Between each mandatory fifteen-minute walk-through of the unit, I often sat down at tables and talked to inmates or watched them play games. I did this more often than most of my fellow officers, but most of us did it at least occasionally. Not surprisingly, those officers who avoided interacting with the inmates had the most difficult time conducting their duties. They also had a much higher burnout rate.

As for me, my interactions with the inmates helped me understand these individuals and their motivations, and this made me far more effective at understanding what was going on, at diffusing situations, and at solving problems.

Perceptions Matter

Our understanding is correlative to our perception.

ROBERT DELAUNAY

The perceptions of the people we serve matter because their perceptions dictate their actions. Being receptive to my surroundings made it possible to gain critical insight that eventually altered my perspective on those perceptions. It taught me to ask myself whether I was reinforcing negative perceptions or giving people reason to question their own perceptions.

For example, during my training time to become a corrections officer at the in-house jail academy, we were taught to carefully prepare our uniforms so that we would be more respected and appear more professional to the inmates. When serving in the military, I'd been stationed at 8th & I in Washington, D.C., in the Ceremonial Unit of the Marines, where I'd learned how to prepare my uniform to the highest level of precision.

My first few weeks as a corrections officer, I prepared my new uniform with this same level of precision, and the reactions of the inmates were interesting. I soon realized they perceived me as arrogant, as though I viewed myself as better than them. Nothing could have been further from the truth, but this was the impression I was giving with my meticulously sharp uniform.

After changing the level of my uniform preparation from razor sharp to merely neat and clean, my uniform no longer stood out in quite the same way. The atmosphere quickly changed too, and the inmates became more respectful to me. Essentially, I had removed a barrier between us, making it easier to do my job.

To be frank, my standards were generally higher than academy standards, but my uniform was an exception. It was simply more important to be approachable than polished, and this included my posture as well as my uniform.

For example, I would generally let my shoulders relax and give off a more laidback attitude, which sent out the message that it was okay to talk to me and I wouldn't be annoyed by it. In contrast, some officers walked around with their chests puffed out, sending the message that they were in charge, basically making it clear that they were above the inmates and unapproachable. In my opinion, this display put a barrier between them and the inmates, making their duties more difficult.

Occasionally, new inmates would test me to see if I was going to enforce the rules, since I looked pretty easygoing, but they quickly learned that I would indeed enforce the rules and that their behavior was going to impact them negatively. Most of the time, other inmates would stop and correct the new inmate before I needed to.

One day early in my career as a corrections officer, I held a discussion with an inmate who wasn't happy that I was holding him accountable for his actions. Inmates at the jail complex were required to make their beds, and one of the most common infractions was not doing so. This particular situation occurred in the afternoon. This inmate had taken a nap and come out to the common area to play a card game without making his bed. When I told him to go make it, he started ranting.

After telling me, "I pay your salary, so really you work for me!" and mouthing off a bit more, he asked in disgust, "Why do you even do this job?"

I briefly considered being a smartass by reminding him that it was county taxpayers who paid my salary and he clearly wasn't one of them, given his current situation, but I remained professional and overcame the urge to degrade or demean him.

Meanwhile, his question of why I do this job stuck with me. I didn't have an answer for him right then, but

I couldn't stop thinking about it. I told the inmate to go back to his cell and calm down, and I gave him the option of additional cleaning duties or being written up for the infraction of disrespect. Extending him a choice showed my respect for him, and it earned me his cooperation that evening and into the future.

That night, during my hour-long commute home, I pondered his question of why I wanted to be a police officer. The next day, I sat down at a table with him and told him I had an answer to his question. I told him this job allowed me to deal with people at their very worst and give them an opportunity for a better future.

Surprised, he said something to the effect of, "Man I was just trippin' yesterday. I didn't expect an answer."

I said, "I know, but I thought you deserved an answer."

"What?" he asked, obviously caught off guard.

"I don't believe you're much different from me," I told him. "We're all just a couple of bad decisions away from wearing someone else's shoes. If I were wearing your shoes, I'd like to know the corrections officer listened and would answer a question when he had a chance."

The inmate gave me a strange look and said I wasn't like most corrections officers.

That's the point of this story and, in a sense, of the entire book. We need to allow the people we serve to relate to us. This would allow them to see past their previous misconceptions of us and would up-end the negative, damaging, and often spiraling interactions we have that lead to additional crimes and sentences. In other words, as I will repeatedly emphasize, we need people to see us as individuals doing a job rather than as bullies in uniforms.

Earning Respect on the Inside

Peace and justice are two sides of the same coin.

DWIGHT D. EISENHOWER

As a corrections officer, I was tasked with the security of my unit and the safety of its occupants. It was my responsibility to hold inmates accountable to the rules while maintaining order. I spent most of my time supervising the inmates and attempting to defuse situations before they escalated out of control. This was a primary objective, but it wasn't always possible.

If asked, I'd have to describe myself as being stricter about enforcing the rules than most of my colleagues. However, once inmates came to know me, they knew I'd be fair and listen. This earned me their respect and was why they seemed to comply much faster with my requests than with the requests of many of my colleagues.

Barking orders is always an option, but making an effort to establish mutual respect usually yields better results. Over the course of time, it became apparent that how I handled people the first time I interacted with them dictated what response I got the next time we crossed paths, if there was a next time.

I learned to constantly ask myself, "Am I handling this situation the best way possible or am I creating a worse problem for later down the road?" Some people think it's easier to gain compliance by force than cooperation, but I disagree. As the next story shows, there's either a price to pay for our actions or there's a reward for them. How I handled this particular case earned me more respect and cooperation from more inmates than I can quantify.

There are two points to this story. One, not everyone wants our help. Two, we are not always aware of our preconceived perceptions of people. To that end, had I not become aware that a particular inmate had a vulnerable side, I never would have solved the gang-related conspiracy that landed him in very hot water.

My supervisor assigned me to a medium security unit consisting of approximately 40 inmates. Supervisors determine assignments, and these can change on a daily basis, depending on the needs of the facility and staffing. Mostly, supervisors try to keep officers in the same units to gain familiarity and achieve consistency with the inmates.

This unit was two levels with a walkway on the second tier that consisted of a grated material that allowed a direct line of sight through it. An inmate was being transferred from the protective custody unit to this medium security unit, and I knew he would not be well received by the inmates here, given the charges against him. Inmates are often placed in protective custody when they're at a higher risk of being assaulted, which is the case for individuals who have committed rape or crimes against children.

This inmate filed an appeal to be removed from protective custody. In protective custody, inmates receive very little time outside their cells, whereas inmates in the general population are allowed out of their cells much more frequently and for longer periods of time. Having won his appeal, this individual was returned to the general population in the medium security unit after lockdown.

The next day, the tension in the unit was palpable, with the brunt of it directed at the new inmate. I soon observed a large country boy with a history of assaulting inmates sitting at a table. When standing, he towered around 6'5" and tipped the scales in the neighborhood of 280 pounds. Three separate people, each representing a gang, joined him throughout the day for a private discussion.

After the evening meal, it was common for inmates to walk laps on the second tier prior to being locked down. This evening had a different feel to it. It was evident something was about to occur. I requested a rover to come to the unit to assist me with observing the inmates and was told an individual would head over as soon as he'd completed his current task.

The tension continued to build with each passing second, so I decided to call the new inmate down to ask what was going on. He responded that nothing was going on. I told him I couldn't help him unless he let me. He replied that he didn't need any help and added a few choice expletives directed at his new inmates. I shook my head, and he returned to walking laps.

A mere five minutes later, an unknown inmate yelled from across the unit, diverting my attention from our new arrival. I looked back just in time to see him stumbling around with a severe injury. He had been struck in the face with such force that his left orbital was fractured. I immediately called a code and ordered the unit to be locked down.

The assaulted inmate was transported to the hospital for treatment, while the aggressor, the 280-pound fellow, was transported to the solitary confinement unit. The assault charge was obvious, but I advised my supervisor that I had all the elements to put together a conspiracy charge as well. I just needed time to confirm my suspicions.

The next day was my day off, but I came in to interview all the people I suspected of being involved. I obtained limited information from the three individuals who had sat down for a private chat with the suspect prior to the assault, but then I went to the solitary confinement unit to interview the suspect.

The beginning of the interview was unproductive. Every question or statement I asked seemed wrong, but I sensed his vulnerability. On instinct, in spite of his record, reputation, and appearance, I looked him right in the eye and said, "Our number one responsibility is to keep people safe. Do you feel safe?"

This giant of a man immediately broke down and sobbed. When he gained control of himself, he explained how everything had unfolded. The three separate gangs had threatened to jump him if he failed to go through with the assault. He'd acted out of desperation and fear.

I filed both the assault charge against the suspect and a conspiracy to commit the crime charge against all three of the gang leaders. Because of how I handled the matter,

I earned a great deal of trust and respect from the rest of the inmates, who knew exactly what had happened.

When Comrades Stray Off Course

*The ultimate measure of a man is not where he stands
in moments of comfort and convenience,
but where he stands at times of challenge and controversy.*

Martin Luther King Jr.

Inmates are not the only problem corrections officers have to deal with. Over time, I discovered that my fellow officers could become as big a hindrance as they could become an asset, and this revelation became an ongoing frustration.

If you find that a fellow officer is making a situation worse, never hesitate to send that individual away. This can be done subtly or directly depending on your relationship with the officer.

For the most part, officers are happy to leave when they aren't needed. I occasionally got some attitude about it, but they always left when I asked them to. Also, I always made it a point to go to the individual later and explain the situation. I always tried to turn the negative into a positive to avoid problems down the road with my fellow officers and also in the hopes that maybe they'd come to see how fruitful my approach was.

That said, had an officer ever refused to leave, I would have asked a supervisor to back up my request.

Diffusing a bad situation will earn you a lot of respect from the member of the public you're dealing with, which in turn promotes increased cooperation. Here are a couple of situations that took me out of my comfort zone and taught me how to deal with my fellow corrections officers who were making tough situations worse or otherwise behaving inappropriately.

I was assigned to a minimum-security unit with a ratio of 180 inmates to three corrections officers, with each officer responsible for 60 inmates in his or her respective unit. The units were in close proximity, and we watched each other's units whenever someone went on break.

One day, an inmate in my unit tipped me off that another inmate was attempting to sell medication for commissary. The inmate tipped me off because he respected and trusted me and didn't agree with the actions of the other inmate.

Inmates are searched whenever they exit and before they enter the unit, so I waited until the inmate went to the gym, since waiting would ensure the medication would remain hidden in his cell. With assistance from the other two officers, I locked the unit down and conducted a search of the cell.

Unfortunately, one officer crashed into the unit, leaving enraged and uncooperative inmates in his wake. There was no excuse for this. He was simply having a bad day and taking it out on the inmates. In short, he was being a jerk. This caused inmates who had been cooperating without issue to stop cooperating, which hindered the investigation and search.

Ultimately, we found pain medication and tattooing implements consisting of a sharpened paper clip, the ink well of a ballpoint pen, and mesh removed from the inmate's property bag. The inmate received new criminal and administrative charges, but I was frustrated that my fellow officer had caused unnecessary aggression and conflict on the unit.

After we completed our search, I spoke privately with him and asked why he'd behaved as he did.

He said something along the lines of, "What does it matter? They're inmates."

I told him I cared because he'd made my job more difficult, and if I ever made his job more difficult, I'd appreciate him letting me know so I could change what I was doing. I spoke respectfully to him, but I gave him something to think about.

During a different shift, I was assigned to the same minimum-security pod with a female officer assigned to the unit next to me. Returning from break, I noticed her leaving a cell, but this wasn't a big deal because we routinely went into cells if something caught our attention.

The next day, a third officer from our team was on break and this same female officer and I were watching his unit. The female officer approached me to ask if she could complete a walk-through of the unit. I gave her permission, and soon I noticed that she entered the same cell as the previous day and remained there a minute of two. This definitely caught my attention. When the third officer returned from break, I decided to question the female officer. She was sitting at her desk hunched over a handwritten note, facing away from the door. At my approach, she desperately attempted to stash the note.

Her behavior cemented my suspicion that she was having an inappropriate relationship with an inmate. Dread filled my stomach to the point that I became nauseated. I knew I had to file a report on her.

Hands down, this was the most difficult report I filed in my short career. I felt like I was betraying one of my own, but I knew that filing the report was the right thing to do. The fact is, we need to police our own people as well as the general population. We need to do the right thing regardless of what some of our peers might think. We are each held to the high standard of being professional and taking appropriate action. When we don't meet this standard, it damages law enforcement's reputation and further taints our relationships with those we supervise.

When I went to my supervisor, I was visibly upset. He asked what was wrong, so I shared my concerns about filing a report on a fellow officer. He stated that this was part of the job and that if my fellow officers couldn't understand that, they should find another profession.

The subsequent investigation determined that the female officer had been having a personal relationship with the inmate for quite some time. She ended up losing her job, but thankfully she hadn't crossed the line sufficiently for criminal charges to be filed against her. If I hadn't done my job, the outcome very likely would have been different.

On another occasion, I was dispatched to a case in which a known criminal had reported a theft. We'd had numerous encounters with this individual in the past, most of which had turned out badly. It was a common practice for other law enforcement to arrive on scene to see if the primary officer needed any assistance, especially when we'd had prior run-ins with certain individuals, and the officer who showed up to assist me had obviously had some negative experiences with this individual in the past.

As soon as the subject saw the officer get out of his vehicle, he stated, "Great, this f***ing guy..." He immediately became confrontational and defensive in his tone and posture.

I told the subject I would be right back, and I met the officer before he approached us.

Upon seeing the subject, the officer's first response, within the man's hearing, was, "What did this shitbag do this time?"

I explained that the individual was reporting a theft, and the officer commented sarcastically that it was funny to see one criminal stealing another criminal's stolen property.

I politely told the officer I didn't need any assistance and asked if he wanted to grab lunch when I was done with the call. He was taken aback at being told he could leave my call, but he agreed to lunch.

I returned to the subject, and his response was, "Thanks, that guy can be a real asshole."

I told him that everyone had the ability to be an asshole under the right circumstances, and he agreed with me. Asking the officer to leave the scene earned me instant respect with the subject and sent the message that I cared about his situation and circumstances.

I then asked him about the crime he was reporting, and he stated, "No, I'm good; it would be a waste of your time."

I said, "Okay, are you sure?" and he answered, "Yeah, I'm good."

Since his demeanor had completely changed and he was being friendly and respectful, I decided to ask for information on anther individual we'd been looking for. He gave me three different locations this acquaintance routinely stayed at.

When I met my fellow officer for lunch, he asked why I'd asked him to leave my call. I explained that his past history with the subject was complicating my current situation with the subject. I also told him that if I ever made his current task more difficult, he shouldn't hesitate to ask me to leave his call because my goal was to be part of the solution, not part of the problem.

The officer then asked what the subject had to say. I told him that he'd decided not to report the crime because he'd be wasting my time. The officer snorted and said, "BS."

I then told him the subject had given me information on the whereabouts of the other criminal we'd been looking for. I knew the officer had been looking for this guy for several weeks.

The officer said, "No way."

I said, "Yeah, as soon as you left, he was my best friend."

Sure enough, the other criminal was arrested about a week later while leaving one of the locations. This interaction improved my working relationship with my fellow officer and increased his insight on how to better do his job.

Earning a Nickname

There is nothing noble in being superior to your fellow man. True nobility lies in being superior to your former self.

ERNEST HEMINGWAY

A "known history" describes a situation in which inmates who have previously been jailed together have an issue with one another. We then place a flag on both inmates as a reminder to keep them separate.

It isn't often that the intake unit misses a known history – it probably happens less than 1% of the time – but quite often when I was on duty, this type of thing happened.

For example, one day I was assigned to the maximum security unit during the introduction of a new inmate. No "keep sep" order was in place, but one look at the new inmate prompted the existing inmate, a hothead and an instigator, to begin tucking his pants into his socks, a clear prelude to a fight. The inmate's rage intensified with each passing second, and I quickly secured the incoming inmate into the visitation room for his safety.

I repeatedly ordered the resident inmate to lock down, but he ignored my orders and continued to rant, so I ordered the entire unit to lock down. The inmate slowly backed up to his cell, still ignoring my commands, so I deployed pepper spray into his face, causing him to stumble backwards into his cell. I called for backup and medical, secured the inmate in his cell, and ensured the rest of the unit was locked down. The inmate contaminated by pepper spray held his cell door shut, preventing medical from assisting him, until an asthma attack caused him to release the cell door. He was then transported to the solitary confinement unit where he was decontaminated in the shower and received administrative discipline for his actions.

As I said, this type of thing happened to me a lot, and my tendency to get into tricky situations was exacerbated by my habit of paying close attention to people's interactions. One day, by listening closely and investigating what I learned, I discovered that several inmates and a convict incarcerated out of state were circumventing our security in the maximum security unit.

I was speaking with two inmates, both of whom were lifelong gang members, or OG's as they're referred to on the street. Inmates like to talk and gossip more than teenagers, and one was bragging about his friend, who was standing next to him.

I acted more interested in the television than in our conversation, responding just enough to keep the inmate talking. He piqued my interest by talking about his friend's son, who was jailed in our minimum security unit, especially when he commented that his friend was in contact with his son.

I wondered how he could be, since we allowed no communication between units, so I nonchalantly inquired about the son.

The inmate stated that the son was doing okay and that "Z" was keeping the father current on his condition.

I had no idea who Z was, but it was obvious he was circumventing our security and enabling communication between units within the jail.

I requested that we send the friend to solitary confinement so we could conduct a search and investigation, and he was transferred that night.

When I searched the inmate's property, I found letters revealing that Z was a convict confined in an out-of-state prison. Z and the father would write each other letters, and then Z would write the son in the minimum unit relaying the information the father wanted passed on.

We pulled the son's property and read his mail, which included letters from Z relaying the father's thoughts. This was basic correspondence from father to son; what was illegal was how our security was being circumvented and compromised by this communication between units. Sure enough, new criminal charges were added to both inmates.

The next day, the original inmate came up to me and asked what had happened to his friend. I shrugged and asked what he thought had happened. He said something to the effect of, "You took our best out of here" and returned to his cell, defeated by the realization that I was more attentive and knowledgeable than I'd let on.

I was affectionately labeled a "shit magnet" after this incident.

Occupational Hazard

That which does not kill us makes us stronger.

FRIEDRICH NIETZSCHE

Conflict can't always be avoided, especially if a subject will not be reasoned with. When you are required to use force, there is always the chance you will be injured in the process. Law enforcement officers accept the risk and do what is required anyway.

One day, I was assigned as a rover to relieve the corrections officer in the suicidal watch unit for lunch. A week earlier, an inmate had broken apart a razor and slit his forearm, cutting himself from wrist to elbow. A few days later, while in the suicidal watch unit, he'd torn open the stitches in a new attempt to take his own life. He was subsequently placed on the highest alert within the unit. This alert restricts the clothing of the inmate to a single blanket and requires the officer on watch to physically witness the inmate breathing every three minutes. We were additionally required to physically see the inmate's arm every three minutes to ensure his safety.

The inmate was sleeping when I came on, so when the three minutes were up, I tapped on the window and asked to see his arm. Begrudgingly, he showed it to me. He then rolled over, again concealing his arm under the blanket.

Three minutes later, I tapped on the window again, requesting to see his arm. He told me, "I just want to sleep," so I told him to keep his arm outside the blanket and I wouldn't wake him up every three minutes. He refused and told me to leave him alone.

I called a supervisor and an additional rover down to the unit. Because the inmate wouldn't cooperate and let us see his arm, we decided to take his blanket.

When the rover and I entered the cell, I told the inmate I needed his blanket. He didn't respond, so we grabbed the blanket, and the fight was on. We took the inmate to the floor to restrain him and then transferred him to a restraint chair.

In the process of taking him to the floor, my right thumb was driven straight into the concrete, tearing a ligament loose from my thumb. We were securing the inmate to the chair when he turned and spit in my face. I turned my head just in time to keep the glob of saliva from hitting my eyes and mouth; it hit the side of my face instead.

The inmate snarled, "How's that for 10 years, bitch?"

He was referring to the additional charges he'd receive for assaulting a peace officer in the act of performing his or her duties.

My injury required surgery, and the doctor signed off on serious bodily injury. Sure enough, the district attorney who pleaded the case added eight years of prison time for the inmate thanks to the assault.

As for me, my professionalism and restraint in not physically retaliating against the inmate earned me the respect of my fellow officers.

Between surgery and recovery, I was off duty for around three months. During this period, I was selected to be a patrol deputy in the patrol division after my oral board and written test were compared to those of other applicants. I returned to full duty just in time to begin training at the in-house academy.

Lesson in What Not to Do

Success depends upon previous preparation,
and without such preparation, there is sure to be failure.

CONFUCIUS

The in-house academy was held Monday through Friday for eight weeks in a classroom setting designed to prepare trainees for field training observation. The academy teaches you the procedures, laws, report writing, investigations, computer training, and expectations involved in doing the job, while field training observation is an extended test to see if you can actually do the job.

Toward the end of the academy, my class was given the opportunity to execute a search warrant on a sexual assault case. There were only six of us in the in-house academy, and we were briefed by the lead detective on the case. That night, the behavior of one of the detectives forever cemented my character as a sheriff's deputy.

The lead detective, a woman, told us that a female had reportedly been raped at a multi-level single family home, but the detective didn't know the room or rooms in which the rape had occurred because the woman was unconscious at the time of the incident. The detective gave us a list of items we were to search for and the address of the residence.

We met at the address and reviewed the search parameters one more time, then filed in against the southern wall inside the living room. We waited there while the lead detective explained the search warrant to the homeowner/suspect.

During that time, another detective strolled into the living room with an I-don't-give-a-shit attitude and plopped down on the sectional sofa in front of us. His cavalier attitude and behavior were disturbing to see. The sectional couch was a faux leather/cloth fabric with visible staining. It was quite possible the woman had been raped on that couch, and he was contaminating the scene.

My fellow trainees shared my view. Our expressions must have been clear, because the detective only sat there a couple of minutes before getting up. I suspect we made him uncomfortable. Later, that same detective stated that he'd searched the laundry room and found nothing, but when another trainee entered the room, he discovered a used condom.

The detective obviously had no interest in solving the case and didn't want to be there, and his attitude and approach hindered our investigation. I told myself that night that I would never be that guy. Whenever I wore the uniform, I would always give my best effort.

Sure enough, the six of us ended up discovering every item on the search warrant. The lead detective was pleased with our work, but this was just the tip of the iceberg. After graduating from the in-house patrol academy, it was time for field training observation, or FTO. This not only tasked us with as many duties and different types of stimulation as possible, but it also took place over a variety of shifts to see how we handled the stress involved with inconsistent sleeping patterns.

Not surprisingly, the washout rate of officers in FTO is much higher than the washout rate of officers in the in-house academy. During FTO, other deputies even give you their calls to give you as much exposure as possible. They want to see you interacting with people, writing reports, making arrests, booking evidence, running code, and all around multitasking.

As a rule of thumb, patrol deputies must be able to drive aggressively (often faster than 100 mph) while reading a computer screen, talking on the radio, coordinating backup and medical, and comprehending the dispatched notices of the individuals involved, including the history, the location, and the circumstances of specific incidents. This allows them to jump into action as soon as they arrive, because seconds can make the difference between life or death.

To say I was up for the challenge would be an understatement. I loved every moment of this complex job. Every experience I had with inmates, my fellow law enforcement personnel, and the general public shaped my approach and cemented my belief that cooperation, not compliance, was a better, more effective, and more humane way to interact with those suspected of breaking the law.

Cooperation versus Compliance

Motivation is the art of getting people to do what you want them to do because they want to do it.

DWIGHT D. EISENHOWER

I have a shirt I like to wear that states, "Hard work pays off in the future; laziness pays off now."

With a bit of reflection, it's easy to see how this statement relates to the concept of cooperation paying off in the future and compliance paying off now. As mentioned earlier, the effort I expended to gain a subject's cooperation usually took less time and effort in the long run than trying to force the individual to comply. The latter approach played into the stereotype of the "asshole cop" and created additional problems that had to be addressed.

By contrast, gaining a subject's cooperation usually paid off in the here and now as well as down the road. Sometimes it even caused suspects to provide assistance that helped me further investigate a case.

A Little Understanding Goes a Long Way

The supreme art of war
is to subdue the enemy without fighting.

SUN TZU

One day, I was dispatched to a reported identity theft at a construction business. Employees at the business told me the victim had come in after being notified by the IRS that he worked for the business and owed taxes.

Turns out, a male employee at the business had been using the victim's name, social security number, and driver's license.

The suspect's driver's license was on file, and when I ran it in the system, I found numerous changes to the man's height, weight, address, phone number, and the date of issue, This is typical of fake IDs, which usually match the physical description of the individual responsible for the identity theft but do not match the Department of Motor Vehicles (DMV) database.

I arrived at the construction site where the suspect was working and asked for his ID. He handed me a Mexican ID that resembled him but identified him by another name. I showed him the copy of the driver's license from his employer and asked for an explanation.

He explained that he had a family and needed to work, so he'd bought the ID and social security number from a flea market.

I told him I could respect that he wanted to work and provide for his family, and this made a big impression on him. My words and tone of voice let him know I wasn't judging him for his actions and more importantly that I cared about him and his family.

After that, he was happy to answer my questions in a very detailed manner, even volunteering information that I hadn't requested. We became two people having an open conversation.

When I asked him where the ID and social security card were now, he told me he'd destroyed them after using them to get the job.

I arrested the suspect, placed him in a belly belt for his comfort, and transported him to jail. Since the flea market was outside my county, I forwarded the case to other relevant jurisdictions and to immigration and filed a police report so the victim could get his tax information corrected.

This case was pretty cut and dried and the suspect was cooperative, but sometimes individuals don't cooperate, at least not initially.

Getting to the Truth

*Peace cannot be kept by force;
it can only be achieved by understanding.*

ALBERT EINSTEIN

I responded to a call to be on the lookout for a reckless driver. Upon locating the vehicle, I pulled it over and asked the driver for his license, registration, and proof of insurance. The driver stated that he did not have his license and handed me his proof of insurance, a temporary 60-day policy that had expired two weeks earlier.

Because I suspected he was being dishonest about his identity, I asked the driver to write out his name, date of birth, social security number, and address. That way, if needed, I'd have physical evidence that he'd lied to me that I could book as evidence. After all, it was impossible for individuals to argue that they hadn't given me the information when I had it in their handwriting.

The driver wrote down a name with a date of birth and social security number and stated that his driver's license was from another state.

Meanwhile, I noted the driver's multiple gang-related tattoos, including spider webbing on his elbows and 88s on his arm. They appeared to be lower-quality tattoos that very well could have been prison tattoos. Knowing what they meant gave me some insight into who I might be dealing with.

In this case, the 88s on the suspect's arm corresponded to HH, which is a white supremacist gang and stands for Hail Hitler. The spider webbing on the elbows indicated the suspect was an enforcer in the gang and consequently likely to be violent. The low quality of the tattoos told me he was probably a convicted felon.

I requested an out-of-state check on the name, date of birth, and social security number he'd given me, and clearance came back with a similar name with the same date of birth but the social security number wasn't listed and could not be confirmed. The driver's license had expired five years earlier and the name was spelled a bit differently. There was also an alias attached to the name.

I tried to confirm that my driver was in fact the person listed out of state in the hopes of confirming one or more previous addresses, and the driver gave me two different addresses. Neither matched the DMV database, nor could he explain why the middle name was different.

After obtaining the contact information for the driver's mother who was reported to be the registered owner of the vehicle, I called and left her a message to call me back, but I didn't hear from her in a timely fashion.

I arrested the driver of the vehicle for driving on an expired license and placed him in the back of my car. While transporting him to the jail complex, he stated, "Okay, I will tell you my real name."

He was in a split cage, so it was difficult to hear him through the cage and over the radio noise. I told him I'd speak with him before we went into the jail, and he was okay with that.

When we arrived, I rolled down his window and stood outside the vehicle to talk to him. I read him his Miranda rights, and the suspect stated that he understood and still wanted to speak with me.

He told me his real name, date of birth, social security number, and the number from his in-state ID card. He stated that he was suspended on an out-of-state driver's license and possibly had a warrant out of an adjacent county. This confirmed my suspicious about his gang and criminal history, and I ran this new information through clearance. I soon learned he was a revoked habitual, with 23 additional actives. He also had a failure to appear warrant out of a local municipality.

I asked him whose information he'd actually given me. If it belonged to a real person, he'd also just committed the crime of identity theft, which is a felony charge.

He said he'd just made up the name and date of birth.

I asked why he'd given me false information, and he said it was because he didn't want to go to jail. I took him into the booking area and had them pull an old booking photo of him from when he'd been incarcerated in the county five years earlier. This photo confirmed his identity.

In the end, I charged the suspect with attempting to influence a public servant, a felony; driving on a revoked license, a misdemeanor; and failure to drive within lane, a traffic offense and the original reason I'd pulled him over.

I gave him numerous chances before I arrested him to give me the correct information. After I arrested him as a different person, it was a little late to cooperate and have the charges dropped.

This case is an example of how an individual who initially didn't cooperate eventually volunteered his true identity. I believe this was a result of how I treated him. Because I didn't call him out for lying or demean him, he volunteered his true identity. If he hadn't, he would have been booked into the jail with his identity in question, and the jail would have needed to do extra work to confirm his identity.

I always tried to educate the people I dealt with so their next encounter with law enforcement could potentially be better. I told him that if he'd simply told me the truth, he could have avoided a felony charge.

He actually thanked me for explaining this to him. Now he was mad about the situation and angry with himself, but he was no longer mad at me. Consequently, I believe his next encounter with law enforcement might possibly be more straightforward.

Whenever I arrested someone, whether it was for a warrant or another crime committed, I always charged the individual for the original reason I'd contacted him, even if it was an equipment violation. That way there was no question in court about the reason for the initial contact. Doing this meant completing an additional form, the ticket, but taking the time to complete the ticket accomplished two things.

First, it made my case stronger, which meant it would be less likely to go to court and be pleaded out. Second, it established my history of contacting and ticketing people for these kinds of violations. This was important, because defense attorneys would otherwise try to claim that I singled out this client, contacting him for something I wouldn't contact anyone else for. Having a record nullified that claim.

Sometimes, as in the next case, I was unable to get a suspect to comply with my commands. Nonetheless, my positive prior encounters with the homeowners paid dividends and allowed me to safely apprehend the felon. This case also illustrates how professionalism and patience win over spectators, even if they happen to be career criminals.

Winning Over Spectators

There is some good in the worst of us and some evil
in the best of us.
When we discover this, we are less prone to hate our enemies.

MARTIN LUTHER KING JR.

At approximately 1:30 in the morning, I received information from a police officer that an individual with a couple of felony no-bond warrants was most likely staying at a residence. The officer wanted to question the individual about a hit and run accident. He knew I had a good rapport with the homeowners, as I'd made multiple warrant and felony arrests from the location, and he wanted me to accompany him.

The residence was a mobile home with video cameras and motion-activated lights on the outside. Through the windows, we could see people moving around and watching TV. I approached the back of the residence and knocked on the door while the other police officer remained on the front side of the trailer.

When the man and woman who owned the home asked who was at the door, I replied that it was Deputy Spencer. At that, they let me in.

I can't emphasize what a huge breakthrough this was. It wasn't something they had to do. They could have told me to leave, and that would have been that. I truly believe their decision to let me in was a result of my previous encounters with them. I'd dealt with them numerous times on narcotics complaints and other calls, but I'd never arrested them, nor had I judged them or spoken down to them. I had always treated them with respect, even though they had a criminal history and we believed they were manufacturing methamphetamines.

Upon entering the residence, I noticed the younger couple sitting on the couch in the living room and that the male homeowner's arm was in a cast. I asked what he'd done to his arm, and he told me he'd been working on the roof when he fell off and broke it.

"That sucks," I said sympathetically.

I asked him this question for a couple of reasons. The first was to let him know I noticed new things, and the second was to get him talking without being defensive.

When I asked about the suspect, the homeowners told me they hadn't seen him in several days. I told them we knew he'd been here the day before and was suspected of pulling into the driveway after a hit and run accident;

I also told them we knew his vehicle had been stored on the property.

The man left the room and went to the southern bedroom, but the woman was still with me, and I introduced myself to the couple on the couch.

Concerned about my safety, the woman leaned towards me. Whispering, she asked if I had anybody else outside like I had in prior incidents.

I advised her that I did, and she whispered in my ear, "Okay, he's in the back bedroom," and motioned to the northernmost bedroom. She then told the couple on the couch they probably needed to move because I was going to search the rest of the trailer and there could be an issue.

For the record, I never punished observers for assisting me, even if they initially lied, like this couple did, as that would have prevented any assistance in the future.

Attached to the northernmost bedroom was a small bathroom and hallway that formed a very tight corridor in the shape of a backwards "L." There was another door into the bedroom by the front door, but it had a mechanical lock on the inside and no door handle. The other officer joined me inside, and I requested officers from another agency go ahead and set up outside the mobile home on the north side.

I addressed the suspect repeatedly through the bathroom doorway while announcing, "Sheriff's Office; I'm Deputy Spencer." The suspect spoke to me and eventually opened the bedroom door enough to allow visual contact. I could physically see him when I was in the bathroom looking in through the door.

The suspect was agitated, paranoid, and jumpy, and his eyes were extremely constricted. I addressed him by name, and he said, "What? That's not my name."

I said, "Okay, what is your name and date of birth?"

He stated that he didn't remember, but I recognized him from the Department of Motor Vehicles photo. The difference was that in that photo, he had hair. The witness in the hit and run accident had advised that the suspect was nearly bald, with tightly clipped hair, and that he was missing teeth. This matched the identity of the person in front of me.

I requested a clear channel and for medical to stage in the area. I was standing in the bathtub in the very small bathroom when the suspect opened the bedroom door. When he slammed the door about five seconds later, I had a very distinct danger sense, and the other officer and I quietly backed out of the bathroom to the hallway.

About the time we got to the hallway, the door briefly sprang open, but when the suspect saw that I wasn't in the bathtub, he slammed the door again. If we hadn't backed out of the bathroom, I believe he would have assaulted us.

We staged in the hallway, which allowed us to look into the bathroom and into the bedroom whenever the suspect opened the door. For approximately 30 to 45 minutes, the other police officer and I tried to talk the suspect out of the bedroom and then the bathroom so we could handcuff him. We repeatedly told him that he was under arrest for the existing warrants, but he would not comply with our commands.

Another deputy arrived on scene and staged next to me. Throughout our interactions, I kept transitioning between my taser and my firearm, depending on the behavior of the suspect. Because I was so patient, the homeowners went from being uncomfortable that we were there – after all, no one likes copes in their home – to yelling at their friend to try to get him to comply. They were upset by his actions and even thanked me for handling the situation so patiently. In fact, at one point, the male homeowner said, "Screw it; you have my permission to kick in the other door," meaning the padlocked one.

The suspect would not move away from the door-frame of the bathroom to the bedroom, and he kept looking at something in the upper portion of the doorjamb and then down about waist level at something inside the bedroom, but we couldn't tell what it was.

Every time we moved our hands, he jumped back. He would not comply with our commands to turn around, put his hands behind his back, and walk backwards toward us.

I transitioned to my handcuffs when the police officer on my right had his firearm drawn and the deputy on my left had his taser out. After medical was staged in the area, we gave the suspect another set of commands. When he did not comply, the deputy tazed him while he was lunging back into the bedroom.

I rushed in while the suspect was falling. He landed between a bed and a dresser on his butt in a halfway sitting position. I was able to get one cuff on his left wrist before the taser finished its five-second cycle and he tightened up and resisted us. We then flipped him face down onto the bed while holding onto the cuff attached to his left wrist. The cuff had not been double locked yet, and it cinched down on his left wrist.

The suspect kept his arms under his body and would not release them. After giving him another taser cycle, we were able to get his hands out from under him and onto his back, and then I was able to apply the right handcuff.

We took the suspect out to the waiting ambulance. He complained that his left handcuff was too tight, so a sheriff's office sergeant on the scene slightly loosened it before double locking it again. The suspect was placed in my patrol car, and I went back inside the residence to thank the homeowners for their patience and for allowing us to handle this difficult situation.

They assured me that the suspect didn't live there; he was just staying the night and had brought some things with him. The woman said she'd felt bad for him because he had no place to go, and she agreed to a search of the northernmost bedroom where the suspect was staying. She also completed a witness statement of the incident that included when the suspect had arrived at the residence.

Normally criminals don't agree to let law enforcement in their homes, much less search their homes, so this was a huge deal.

Our search of the bedroom revealed that the upper doorjamb of the doorway between the bathroom and bedroom concealed a large set of throwing knives; this was what the suspect had kept looking at while talking with us. A large folding knife sat on a set of speakers about waist level right inside the doorway; this was the other item the suspect had been looking at. We also found multiple meth pipes on top of a cabinet on the western wall of the bedroom. There were several other knives in the bedroom and multiple baggies with small amounts of clear white residue on the counter along with syringes and more baggies with white crystal powder in the uppermost right dresser drawer under the cabinet on the western wall.

The northern window was covered with multiple blankets that the suspect had put up; the homeowner advised us that none of the knives or drugs had been in the residence prior to the suspect's arrival.

As soon as the suspect was in custody and being transported to the ambulance to have the probes from the taser removed, I let the dispatchers know that all law enforcement personnel were okay.

Dispatchers have a very stressful job. While they are not on scene for volatile situations, they are concerned about the first responders they dispatch and are usually left waiting to assume the worst. This is why I frequently made it a point to message my dispatchers to thank them and include them in my investigations.

Not surprisingly, I had a great relationship with my dispatchers, who assisted me countless times. Often when I was driving to a scene, I asked them to do a history search of people or a location. They also requested photos on my behalf, confirmed warrants, organized other agencies, and validated revoked statuses. I was very thankful for my dispatchers. They were my lifelines when I needed assistance.

I transported the suspect to the hospital for a jail clearance and was relieved by another deputy, who remained with the suspect for the clearance and transported him to the jail complex. The suspect was arrested on multiple felony warrants and additionally charged with resisting arrest, possession of a weapon by a previous offender, possession of narcotics, and possession of drug paraphernalia. The police department also closed its case on the hit and run accident.

The suspect didn't willingly cooperate, but the homeowners did. Thanks to the relationship I'd developed with them, I was able to arrest the suspect without anyone getting hurt.

Cooperation, not compliance, always works better in the end, but it isn't always possible to gain cooperation. Sometimes that's a luxury you just don't have, as was the case in the following example, when I couldn't call for help and was forced to act quickly and alone.

Desperate Situation

Though force can protect in emergency, only justice, fairness, consideration, and cooperation can finally lead men to the dawn of eternal peace.

DWIGHT D. EISENHOWER

One of the most dangerous and infuriating situations I ever experienced occurred when I was dispatched to a disturbance in progress call at a residence and my equipment failed.

A neighbor had called the police after hearing a disturbance next door and a woman screaming, "Get off of me!"

When I arrived on scene, the front door was open. I saw a distraught female who appeared to have injuries to her arms. She looked right at me and made eye contact, then dropped her head and began to shut the front door.

I will never forget the look this woman gave me. It was the most defeated look I had ever seen. Her expression and body language screamed, "I am going to die now, and that is okay with me."

I called for her to come out of the house, but she shut the door and locked it before I could get to the front door.

I knocked on the door and got no response. I attempted numerous times to inform dispatch of the situation, but my radio traffic was broken or toned out completely.

I banged on the door, identified myself, and asked the woman to open the door, but there was no response.

My stress was so great that I deferred to using military terminology and requested a secure channel instead of a clear channel. They mean the same thing, but the equipment wasn't working properly, and I couldn't tell if the channel was cleared or not.

CHAPTER 3: Cooperation versus Compliance

I attempted to tell dispatch that I was going to attempt entry and then yelled one more time, "Sheriff's office. Open the door or I'm coming in!"

My handgun was drawn and at the low ready.

Just as I was about to move, the woman opened the door. I requested that she come outside, and she identified herself as a local police officer arrived on the scene. I advised her to walk over to the police officer around the corner in front of the garage, and she complied.

I announced that anyone else in the house should come out now, and a man in a black shirt torn around the neck came to the door. I told him to come out on the porch, and he complied. He identified himself with a name and date of birth. He had scratches on the front of his neck that led onto his chest and was very aggressive in his demeanor and tone of voice.

I instructed him to sit down in a chair on the front porch as three other police officers arrived on scene. They had seen the call on the screen but had only received garbled transmissions from me. Two remained outside to watch the man while the other police officer and I searched the rest of the residence. No one else was there, and nothing looked especially out of place.

I went back out to speak with the woman, who was visibly shaking. She had bruising beginning on both arms and numerous small scratches. One of the police officers left the scene, since it was under control, while we continued to attempt to clear the parties. Finally, one of the police officers discovered that the woman had a protection order and was the protected party.

I told the man he had one more chance to tell me his real name and date of birth. He told me who he was, and sure enough, he was the restrained party in the protection order.

I asked him what had happened, and he stated that he'd had a disagreement with his girlfriend, whom he'd been dating and sleeping with off and on for the past two years. I asked specifically about his injuries, and he stated that the scratches were old and that he'd cut himself shaving. I indicated the scratches on his chest, and he stated he must have cut himself shaving there as well. The check on him came back with two valid warrants.

I went back to speak with the woman and noticed that her neck was starting to swell. I asked if he'd choked her, and she didn't answer. She agreed to meet with a victim advocate, and I requested an advocate and paramedics by radio, which was now working.

The woman stated that she was getting out of the shower right before the altercation occurred. She said that she'd scratched him when he got on top of her and forcibly held her down. She stated that it hurt when he held her down. I asked if he'd raped her, and she dropped her head and meekly stated no. I asked if she had clothes on when he was on top of her, and she hesitated and said yes.

I believe the woman was raped. I also believe that if I'd had the opportunity to gain her cooperation, she might not have lied to me about that specific crime. As it was, she was too afraid to tell me the truth. In that regard, forcing my way in damaged the investigation and my ability to arrest the suspect on all the counts I believe he was guilty of, but under the circumstances, I'd had no choice but to force compliance. This was a situation of imminent danger. Because the woman's safety was compromised, I'd had to act.

I arrested the suspect, put him in a belly belt for comfort, and placed him in the back of my patrol car. The woman went back inside the residence with one of the police officers and asked to be notified when the suspect was released. A bit calmer now, she sat down at the table to complete her information.

When paramedics and firefighters arrived and came into the residence, she took one look at them and began curling into a fetal position. The fact that the men coming into her home, firefighters in particular, physically repulsed her was another indication that she'd been sexually assaulted. I told one paramedic he could come in and escorted everyone else out of the residence.

I eventually learned that the suspect had been convicted of a protection order violation before. This was important, because it changed the classification of the charge from a class two misdemeanor to a class one misdemeanor, with its correspondingly more harsh sentencing range.

This case will always stick with me for a couple of reasons. First, I was enraged that my equipment didn't function properly when I needed it most. I'd been a split second away from forcing entry into a residence by myself, and I couldn't even tell anyone what I was doing. Functioning equipment and appropriate backup would have significantly lowered my stress level. As it was, I was full on, ready to take care of business. My posture and tone meant one thing – I was going to take decisive action, and I was going to take it now.

Had more of us been there, I could have been slightly less aggressive. In turn, maybe the woman would have been less taken aback when she opened the door. Nonetheless, we still would have been required to act quickly given the circumstances. My body produced so much adrenaline in response to this situation that I began physically shaking once the incident was complete.

Second, I will never forget the look the woman gave me when she saw me. To this day, I have never seen a more defeated individual. She was ready to die and had no more fight left in her. Fortunately, she didn't die.

Otherwise her face would have haunted me instead of being a reminder to never quit or give up.

Sometimes we aren't afforded the luxury of gaining cooperation, but most of the time, cooperation is achievable and positively affects everyone involved. That said, sometimes we find ourselves in complex situations that require us to make decisions in a sea of grey.

When Blue Lines Become Grey

What lies behind us and what lies before us are tiny matters compared to what lies within us.

OLIVER WENDELL HOLMES

The safety of the public is law enforcement's number one priority, with the safety of law enforcement personnel a close second. Many decisions and actions are taken based on some level of concern for safety. Unfortunately, some of those decisions and actions have to be determined in fractions of seconds. In such cases, blue lines sometimes become grey.

To Shoot or Not to Shoot?

Service to others is the rent you pay for your room here on earth.

MUHAMMAD ALI

I once had to make a split second decision while serving a mandatory protection order with a kick-out. This means I was going to an individual's home, serving him with a protection order, and making him leave his home, all within roughly 15 minutes.

The protection order was a no-contact order with an added clause that the individual could not own or possess any firearms. The individual in this case had a criminal history of violence and gang activity that I was aware of before making contact.

I knocked on the individual's door in the morning, waking him up. When he came to the door, I saw that he was about six feet tall and weighed over 300 pounds. He was wearing shorts and a tank top and had numerous visible gang-related tattoos. He was not fully awake or alert yet, and after I introduced myself, he invited me into the singlewide trailer house. We walked down a narrow hallway to the main bedroom.

I stopped at the door of the bedroom and looked inside. The room was very cluttered, and the oversized bed took up most of the space. The man's girlfriend was sitting in the far corner of the room. To my right was a dresser, and on top of it was a pistol pointing in my direction. I could tell from the bore size that it was either a BB gun or a pellet gun, neither of which is classified as a firearm.

I explained the protection order and kick-out along with the stipulation that he not own or possess any firearms. The protected party in this case was another woman, not the man's girlfriend.

Without warning, the man turned and pulled another pistol out from under the pillow. I saw it in the gap between his side and arm as he turned back to face me. He was holding it by the base of the handle with it dangling upside down between his thumb and index finger.

If his hand had been wrapped around the grip of the pistol in a normal fashion, I would have drawn my gun and shot him in the head with little to no warning. Even without his hand wrapped around the grip of the pistol, I would have been completely justified in shooting and killing him, but I'm thankful I made the decision not to take his life. In this case, it was the correct choice.

As he finished turning toward me, he explained, "It's just a bb gun." He wanted to know if he could take his bb guns with him when he left.

I stated that he could because bb guns were not classified as firearms. I then explained how close I'd come to shooting and killing him.

He was taken back and apologetic. Still half asleep, he hadn't considered what he was doing. I told him never to reach for a gun without telling the officer beforehand, and I hope he remembers my words. He was very fortunate this day, and he might not be so fortunate again.

It Takes a Special Kind

Whoever fights monsters should see to it that in the process he does not become a monster.

FRIEDRICH NIETZSCHE

It takes a special kind of individual to become a member of law enforcement, in part because people often distort events or facts to paint a more favorable appearance of themselves and the situation they're in. As a point of public insight and awareness, officers of the law are lied to approximately 80% of the time but not necessarily by 80% of the people.

I believe the overall problem originates from the difficulty of relating to the work we do. Most jobs allow for a fairly clear understanding of what is required on an hourly, daily, or weekly basis, but law enforcement officers have no idea what the next hour will bring. One minute we can be on a routine call, and the next minute we hear about a disturbance in progress, shots that have been fired, or an accident with injuries, and we must take action to preserve life.

In addition, imagine for a second that the vast majority of people at your job hate you and become aggravated at the mere sight of you. How would you handle being lied to 80% of the time? How long would you remain at your job?

As this next story shows, because law enforcement is so poorly understood and because people are frequently uncooperative and antagonistic, it requires a special kind of person to answer the call. Here's my advice on dealing with irrational people: remain calm and professional and keep asking for clarification. This may not sway the individual, but it will gain you the support of bystanders who will then view the individual as the one who is out of line.

This case involved a cold theft at a single-family residence. "Cold" means the crime has already occurred and isn't in progress. This case highlights the importance of addressing the initial perceptions and reactions of individuals involved while somehow maintaining the patience and persistence to calmly and professionally do your job, something that is more easily accomplished in theory than in practice.

When I arrived at the residence, I spoke with the home-owner, who stated that the day before, he'd realized some tools were missing out of his unlocked van. This incident reminded him that a week earlier, he'd come home to find his gate open. He'd checked his surveillance cameras, which revealed a young white male at the back of the residence. Another camera showed the same individual loading something into a darker colored sedan with unreadable plates parked next to the van. Another angle showed the vehicle quickly exiting the driveway without stopping to close the gate.

The homeowner believed he knew who the suspect was. I asked him how certain he was, and he said very sure. I asked how he knew this individual, and he said the man had worked for him around Christmas doing a few odd jobs and that he didn't have any tools of his own.

The homeowner stated that the individual also worked at a magazine across the street from the post office in a nearby town and lived with a lady twice his age who owned the magazine.

The homeowner had a lengthy missing property list to complete, so I asked him to work on that while another deputy and I drove separately to the magazine to attempt to contact the suspect. I arrived first and walked inside. A woman approached and asked if she could help me.

I was holding a piece of paper in my hand with the individual's name on it, and I raised it and stated that I needed to speak with the man. She took the paper out of my hand and said, "Okay. Let's talk outside."

I said that was fine and followed her outside.

She asked why I needed to talk to the individual, and I told her it was in reference to a theft case. She asked me about the theft, and I told her I couldn't speak to her about it because it was under investigation.

She asked for my business card and said she would have the man give me a call. I asked where he was, and she stated that he was working. I asked where, and she became irritated and said, "I told you; he's working."

I said I understand and that I was working as well and attempting to do my job. I asked her where the individual lived, and she started yelling at me and told me I was being very offensive.

About this time, the other deputy arrived on the scene.

I calmly stated, "Ma'am, I don't understand how I'm being offensive."

She yelled, "You're being an asshole and offensive!" Then she yelled, "Do you have a warrant? You need a warrant! You need to leave right now!" She raised her smart phone and stated that she was recording me and kept it about 18 inches away from my face.

I calmly advised her that we were on public property and that I did not need a warrant; I just needed to talk to the individual we were looking for. I again calmly asked where the individual lived, and she yelled, "You're an asshole, and I'm not telling you!"

I calmly stated, "Okay. What is your name, ma'am?"

She yelled, "You are offensive and an asshole and don't have a warrant!"

She was worked up to the point that droplets of spit came out of her mouth. One hit me on the forehead, and a second hit me on my cheek.

I raised my voice so she could hear me over all her yelling and stated, "If you spit on me again, I will arrest you."

She yelled, "I didn't spit on you!" She turned her head and spit on the ground, then yelled, "That is spitting!"

About this time, I requested that a police officer in town respond to my location. I wanted to see if he knew the individual or this lady.

The woman was now yelling, "What? I can't call you an asshole without you threatening to arrest me?"

My commander knew something was up – I was requesting an additional unit when I already had another deputy with me – and called me on my cell phone.

I answered but didn't have time to say anything before the woman yelled, "What are you going to do, shoot me? Oh wait, never mind; I'm not black!"

The commander asked me to give him a call when I was done, and as I hung up, the woman began yelling again.

"I asked you for a business card, and you're being an asshole and threatening me!"

I calmly reached into my pocket and pulled out a business card, which she yanked out of my hand.

I calmly told her, "I need that piece of paper." It contained the notes for the case that she had taken from my hand earlier.

She said, "No, you gave it to me."

I replied, "No, you took it out of my hand, and I need that piece of paper."

She stated, "I am not going to give it to you."

I said sternly, "Ma'am, if you don't give me the piece of paper, I will arrest you for not following a lawful order of a peace officer."

She handed me the piece of paper and stormed into the business.

While I waited on the sidewalk for the local police officer to arrive, the woman exited the business with a companion, saw me, snorted, and went back inside. A couple of minutes later, she came around the corner driving an older blue Mercedes with an in-state plate that came back with her name and address. She lived in town but on the adjacent county side.

About this time, the police officer arrived on the scene. I walked over to speak with him as a man came out of the business. He quietly and respectfully walked up and told the officer and me that he'd been told to trespass us from the property. Together, the other officer and I advised him that he could not trespass law enforcement from a place of business. The man identified himself and handed me a business card, and I asked if the lady always yelled and caused a scene.

"Oh yes," he said, adding, "we just put up with her." He put his personal cell phone on his card in case anyone needed to ask him any questions about her.

He stated that he knew the individual we were asking about but hadn't met him personally. He said this individual sometimes helped at the magazine and delivered some routes. I thanked him for his time and demeanor before accompanying the officer to the woman's address in an attempt to contact the individual.

There was no answer at the door, so I returned to the residence where the theft had occurred to get the homeowner's remaining contact information along with the property list.

An explosion call came at this time that I needed to respond to, but later that day, another deputy offered to go over to the cold theft, get the property list, and enter the items since I was busy investigating the explosion.

A call requesting contact came in while I was on the perimeter of the explosion; it was the suspect in the theft case requesting a call.

Dispatch attached me to the call, and I dialed the number.

A lady answered the phone, and I recognized her voice from my encounter with her earlier. She immediately asked if I was another officer, and I said, "No, Ma'am."

With an aggressive tone in her voice, she said, "Well, who is this?" and I calmly responded, "Deputy Spencer."

She stated that the commander had advised her that they could deal with someone other than me. I calmly stated that I was not aware of that, and she said, "But we will talk to you."

I stated, "No, Ma'am. If the commander told you someone else would handle it, then someone else will handle it."

I apologized for the call and disconnected the phone, and that was the end of my involvement with this challenging case. I'd like to be able to say this type of interaction was rare, but in fact it was fairly common. It highlights how difficult it is to remain patient with people who are immediately antagonistic and doing their best to put you on the defensive.

The fact is, it takes a special type of person to overcome the urge to respond negatively. It's almost impossible to resist this urge if you aren't at peace with yourself. If you are comfortable and confident with yourself, it won't affect you when people act in this manner. If you aren't at peace with yourself, antagonistic people will get under your skin, and you may proceed in a way that causes more problems than it solves.

Most Folks Meet Us on Their Bad Days

When you have a problem, rules don't solve your problem. It's caring and education.

JIM BROWN

People are people. We all have hopes, dreams, struggles, ambitions, desires, and problems. We all have good and bad days. In law enforcement, we deal with a lot of people who are in the middle of a problem and having a bad day. How we do our jobs determines whether their day gets worse or begins to improve. Since I went into law enforcement to help people, it was always a priority for me to remember that, by definition, the folks I had to arrest were having a bad day.

Even though laws are written in black and white to clarify what's right and wrong, enforcing the laws isn't always as straightforward as it sounds. We officers of the peace are sometimes required to determine their meaning, what they pertain to, and what action is required to uphold them. Often, our interpretation of the law determines what actions we do or do not take. In many cases, we must decide whether to issue a citation, make a physical arrest, or place someone on a hold.

We have to make difficult decisions about complicated situations in a relativity short period of time, and we often have discretion regarding whether or not to arrest someone. That said, in cases involving domestic violence that discretion is taken away. The statue says that you shall make an arrest if you have evidence that a crime of domestic violence has been committed. The word "shall" removes the discretion.

With a domestic violence crime, a mandatory no-contact protection order is automatically put in place. I am thankful that in the following case, the courts immediately modified the protection order so that the suspect could have contact with her husband and say goodbye to him. He died in the hospital less than a week after he was admitted. I believe the suspect in this case was fundamentally a good person who made a mistake.

I believe she and her husband were both having a bad day and that she got frustrated with him and hit him. I do not believe she caused him significant injury. This was the only case I ever worked on that made me regret having to do my job. I will always remember it because it was the one time I was required to arrest someone that it didn't feel like the right thing to do.

Upon being dispatched to a medical call at this couple's residence, the paramedics on the scene mentioned that urine had completely saturated the floor. They said the homeowner said her dogs had done it, but when asked about them, she said they'd been dead for quite some time. This was an odd reply, but I figured she was confused with everything that was going on.

The medical call was for the woman's husband, who had reportedly fallen during a seizure and possibly hit his head. He was unresponsive and only slightly able to assist us with moving and loading him on to the gurney. He was transported to a local hospital, whereupon I cleared the call and assumed my involvement in the case was over.

A few days later, I was dispatched to a cold assault contact by phone at the same address. The son of the man in the hospital was the reporting party. He stated that his stepmother had told him she'd had an altercation with her husband prior to our arrival the day of the medical incident. The husband had been pissing and shitting everywhere, and she'd ranted that nobody should have to put up with this and she wasn't going to put up with it anymore. The husband had struck her on the chin after having what appeared to be a stroke. In response, she'd struck him with a closed fist in the side of the head.

When I asked about the incident, the wife reiterated that her husband had struck her after having what she thought was a stroke. At the time, he wasn't wearing any pants or underwear. She stated that she'd struck him on the arm and he'd responded "Ow." When I asked why she'd struck him, she said it was because she wanted to get him dressed before paramedics arrived and he wouldn't cooperate.

When I questioned her again about the urine-saturated carpets, she stated that the urine was from the dogs. I asked where the dogs were, and she again said the last one had died over a year ago. I confronted her on the discrepancy of having wet carpet with no animals in the house for a year, and she stated that she'd cleaned up messes from her husband in the laundry room and elsewhere but wasn't aware that he'd urinated on the carpet.

She told me she had gone to her mother's home in a nearby city after her husband was hospitalized. I told her I would need to come down and get a written statement from her, and she agreed to meet with me.

I contacted the on-call district attorney by phone after speaking to the woman in the hopes of doing a special filing, and he informed me that this wasn't possible since it was a case of domestic violence, albeit dual domestic violence, since they'd struck each other. I was trying to avoid having to physically arrest the woman, but the domestic violence aspect meant I had to take appropriate action.

I requested that dispatch have local police officers meet me on scene since the location was outside my jurisdiction. Two officers met me as requested, and the wife invited us in and completed a written statement that included the incident in which her husband had struck her and she'd hit him back. He was a stage four cancer patient with multiple other medical conditions, including diabetes. These conditions made him an at-risk adult, and she was his caregiver.

Many details are excluded from reports because the information isn't relevant, but the following details reveal how law enforcement is often treated and how this can complicate an already challenging situation.

The wife's mother, who was extremely mean, was at the residence as well. She was around 90 years old, maybe 80 pounds total in weight, and using a large walker to get around the house. While I was talking with the wife, my attention diverted, the mother became very aggressive towards me and began picking up her walker like it was a weapon. She could barely lift it, so she began cursing at me.

The male officer watching this situation unfold stepped between us and became stern with the old lady, who then threatened him as well. The female police officer who answered the call with us attempted to calm down the mother, who proceeded to call her every name in the book. I was convinced one of us was going to be assaulted by the mother and decided ahead of time not to respond with force. She wouldn't be able to generate much force herself, and any force I used could easily hurt her. Turns out we weren't assaulted physically, though we certainly received a terrible tongue lashing.

After I conducted my investigation and the wife completed her written statement, I arrested her at the residence. She wasn't in good health herself, so I took her medication and cane with me so the medical staff at the jail would be aware of her needs. I handcuffed her in front of her body for comfort but couldn't use a belly belt because it wouldn't fit around her. I buckled her into the back seat of my patrol car before transporting her to the jail complex.

After advising her grown children of the situation, I photographed her right wrist where a bruise was present from striking her husband; I did not observe any injuries on her chin. No victim advocate was requested or called for because her husband was unresponsive and expected to enter hospice soon.

The district attorney's office reached the same conclusion I did and dropped the charges against the wife. I was grateful, but I still regret having to arrest her. I don't believe she was physically able to generate enough force to do any damage, but this case speaks to the letter of the law and not to justice. I knew from the beginning what had to be done. I also knew it wasn't the right thing to do, which is why I took the extra step of contacting the DA to attempt a special filing.

Try to Understand the Victim

There's a way to do it better – find it.

THOMAS A. EDISON

It also helps to know and understand your victims and to try to view the situation from their perspective. One particular case was extremely unique and required me to do a fair amount of research while keeping the victim's needs in mind.

After getting the call, I remember returning to the sheriff's office and walking toward the building. One of my deputy bureau chiefs was in his vehicle. He saw that I was in deep contemplation and called me over to ask what was going on. I explained that a venerated object, a Native American sweat lodge, had been desecrated at a residence.

He stated that in several decades of law enforcement, he'd never been involved in a case like this, and he wanted to know how I was going to proceed.

I told him the first thing I was going to do was determine that I actually had jurisdiction on the case. Typically, law enforcement does not have jurisdiction on a Native American Reservation, but the sweat lodge was not on a reservation. Since it is the equivalent of a church, jurisdiction in my state goes to the sheriff's office. After confirming that I had jurisdiction, I was going to investigate the case as a hate crime.

Once jurisdiction was confirmed and I arrived at the residence, I spoke with the reporting party, a Native American holy man, about the incident. He took me to the desecrated sweat lodge in the back corner of his pasture.

The dome-shaped structure was partially covered by a torn and slashed green canvas and had been destroyed in a manner consistent with someone who knew what it was. The directional poles had been manipulated or knocked over. The blanket at the entrance had been placed on top of the stones in the pit. The sacred food had been torn down and placed on a log. The monetary value of the tarp was only $50.00, but the spiritual damage was incalculable. Everyone on scene was upset over the destruction, describing the sweat lodge as a sacred object connected with their spiritual beliefs.

I photographed a partial shoe print on top of the canvas and then cut out and collected that section of canvas. Because this appeared to be a bias-motivated crime, I also conducted an area check by speaking to several neighbors, including two young adults, a man and a woman, who lived next door to the sweat lodge.

Both individuals were uncomfortable speaking with me and declined any knowledge of the existence of the sweat lodge, even though it was easily visible from their property. They were the primary suspects, but the case had to be suspended until further leads developed.

I thoroughly documented this case and all the evidence so that if the suspects committed another crime, something that is very common in bias-motivated crimes, it would be easy to link the crimes and possibly solve this one.

This case reminded me that it isn't what I know but what I can prove that matters. Law enforcement has to meet the burden of proof when writing search warrants or making arrests. I carefully explained the situation to the victims so they were aware of the efforts I'd made and how those efforts would assist us if something similar happened again. In spite of the fact that we didn't solve the case, they were very appreciative of my efforts.

Trying to Sort It All Out

We adore chaos because we love to produce order.

M. C. ESCHER

Sometimes it seemed like I spent most of my time just trying to figure out what was going on and whether or not a crime had actually been committed. Occasionally, situations were complex to the point of being almost impossible to understand. I guess that is the true point and value of law enforcement – our ability to clarify complex if not impossible-to-understand situations and take appropriate action.

This was the case when a woman came into the station to report an assault on her four grandsons, who ranged in age from six to 13 years old. The reported assault had occurred two days earlier at their residence. All told, this case involved two parents, one grandparent, and seven children, one of whom was 18.

The grandmother had picked up the boys in another city the previous day in order to care for them while their father was on vacation with his wife. This family was the modern equivalent of the Brady Bunch. He was the father of all the boys, and she was the mother of all the girls.

When the boys got into the car, they told the grandmother that their stepsister had assaulted them two days earlier. The grandmother saw bruises on a couple of the boys, including bruising on the six-year-old around his right ear and a mark on the right shin of one of the other boys.

I recognized the boys. Just two days earlier, I'd interviewed the father and his sons at their residence. The father had called to complain that his kids were stealing from each other and to ask if he could press charges. He'd explained that his stepdaughter had received a bouquet of flowers made of money. He believed his six-year-old son might have taken some of it, and one of the other kids might have taken some as well.

I'd explained to the father that we had to have a specific person to press charges against and that the person had to be of legal age to commit a crime. Then I'd talked to the boys and explained why it was important to be honest with me and that it could affect their futures, but none of the boys owned up to stealing the money.

At the time, I'd noted how withdrawn the boys were, particularly the youngest. Curled up in a ball between his father's legs, he would not make eye contact with me even when I spoke directly to him. The older boys were more talkative but visibly distressed, and the oldest boy was especially quiet. When I asked him specific questions about his siblings, he became noticeably uncomfortable and painstakingly avoided making eye contact.

The father told me his household was experiencing a bed bug problem and advised me not to enter the residence. He also told me he was getting more and more frustrated with the ongoing problem of his boys assaulting each other and stealing. He stated that Social Services had been in contact with them several times.

My sense was that this father was attempting to do what was right for his children but was in over his head. I noted five cases from the previous year connected to the family. I told him about a program called Youth in Conflict and gave him the contact information.

It's important to note that I went out on this call even though I knew no criminal charges would be filed. I could have told him over the phone that this wasn't a criminal case and to contact Social Services again, but since he was asking for help, I wanted to at least try to help.

The demeanor of the boys told me there was more to the story, but I wasn't sure what to do beyond forwarding my report to Social Services. If I were to have this call again, I would separate the boys and ask to speak to them without their father present. Understanding the present situation better always promotes a more complete report, and this can pay off down the road.

Now, two days later in the station with their grandmother, the boys were noticeably different. They all recognized me and were happy, laughing, and joking.

The six-year-old who wouldn't speak to me before was friendly and talkative and even said, "Hi, how's it going?"

I interviewed each boy individually and another deputy took photographs. When the boys weren't being interviewed, they were happy to sit at the conference table drawing pictures.

The grandmother was present during all the interviews. She was upset at the boys' living conditions and at the actions that had been taken against them, but she was quiet and didn't attempt to influence them.

During his interview, the six-year-old told me he'd been slapped and punched with both an open hand and a closed fist approximately five times by his oldest stepsister. He said that she kicked and kneed him in the buttocks as well and then forced him along with the other three boys to maintain the pushup position until their father came home.

While he was in the pushup position, the six-year-old said the stepsister stepped on his back and hands. He stated that one of his brothers was kicked in the right leg and hit in the back of the head with an open hand by the stepsister.

In his interview, one of the other brothers stated that all the boys had been horsing around in the house and jumping on their beds. He stated that he'd been kicked in his left side in the ribs and in his left leg. He also confirmed that the stepsister had stepped on the youngest brother's hands and back while they were in the pushup position. He confirmed that the stepsister had kicked his other brother in the right calf.

A third brother confirmed that his brother was punched in the head. He stated his oldest stepsister had kicked him in the right calf and kicked his other brother in the ribs and leg. He also mentioned that the stepsister hit the youngest brother in the back of the head with an open hand. He also said the stepsister locked the six-year-old in the garage whenever he cried.

I asked why the boy might be crying, and he said it was because the boy was hurt or scared. When the boy was locked in the garage, the lights would be turned off, and one of the stepsisters would go outside and bang on the main garage door to scare him.

I interviewed the youngest child a second time, and he confirmed that one of his brothers had been hit and kicked and that the other brothers were also kicked. When I asked about the garage, he became more withdrawn and agitated, similar to his demeanor two nights earlier.

I asked the boy if he could get out of the garage on his own or turn the lights on. He said he was too short to turn the lights on, but he could get out of the garage and back in the house if the door weren't locked, but usually it was. He couldn't open the main garage door because it was broken.

After the interviews, I called the father on his cell phone to inform him that the boys and their grandmother were at the station. When I told him the grandmother was reporting an assault, he became very agitated. He seemed more upset about the report than about the welfare of his sons. He instantly started making excuses for the oldest stepdaughter and said the boys were out of control. He also said the bruises hadn't been there before and implied that someone else must be responsible for them. He wondered out loud if he needed to return from his vacation.

I said this was up to him and told him the boys were safe with their grandmother. To my surprise, since he was the person who had authorized her to keep them, the father said he wanted to file kidnapping charges against the grandmother because she wouldn't let him talk to the boys.

I explained to the grandmother that she needed to let the boys talk to their father, and she agreed. A few moments later, I observed the oldest boy on the phone, and once again he was noticeably quiet, guarded, and withdrawn.

After clarifying that the boys would remain with their grandmother through Monday, when it would be determined whether or not they would return home with their father, I told the father that if the boys did return home, the oldest stepsister should not be in the residence until the courts or Social Services determined the appropriate course of action.

Two days later, the mother of the girls, the oldest stepsister, and next oldest stepsister came to the station to be interviewed. The oldest stepsister, age 18, stated that she was rarely home and didn't babysit much. I asked who was responsible for the kids, and she said the girls took care of themselves and the oldest boy was in charge of the boys. It took three separate interviews to get an accurate account of the incident, as she changed her story several times.

She said she'd gotten a ride home after learning that some of her graduation money had been stolen. She said she came into the house and yelled for all the boys to come upstairs, and when she saw the oldest boy, she "freaked out." She said he pushed her and kicked her in the shin, so in self-defense, she punched and slapped him and then yelled at the boys to get into the pushup position. She tried to get the youngest boy to stand in the corner, but he just rolled into a ball and started crying. When the boys were in the pushup position, she walked around them and might have stepped on the youngest boy's hands by accident.

She said that when the father got home, he started yelling at the oldest boy and picked him up by his right ear, bent him over the ottoman, and gave him the worst spanking she had ever witnessed with a paddle he kept for this purpose. She said the father also punched and ground his fist into the boy's leg while telling the boys they were going to be arrested and taken to jail. All this time, the stepsister said she continued to yell at the oldest boy.

At some point during this episode, the father ripped his shorts and went downstairs to change them. While he was downstairs, the oldest stepsister said she freaked out again and attacked and punched the oldest boy. She stated that her younger sister had to pull her off of him.

The oldest stepsister also admitted that an incident occurred in which the youngest boy was locked in the garage with the lights out. During this time, her younger sister banged on the door with the sole purpose of scaring the child.

I interviewed the younger sister next. At first, she wasn't truthful because she was afraid her older sister would go to jail, but after I explained that she wasn't going to jail, she confirmed most of the story. She stated that she'd had to pull her older sister off the oldest boy and that her sister had said he was lucky she'd been pulled off. She also confirmed hearing her sisters talk about the youngest boy in the garage, and she agreed that this was the maddest she'd ever seen the father. She too thought the spanking the oldest boy had received was excessive.

Next I interviewed the mother of the girls, who downplayed the issues in the home. She even stated that the household was quiet. When I asked who caused the most trouble in the house, she stated that it was the six-year-old boy.

All told, I had to analyze five separate stories before I could draw conclusions or take next steps. This included determining which acts were committed for disciplinary purposes. The fact is, the child abuse statute gives a lot of leniency for acts of discipline. Locking the six-year-old in the garage was horrific, and I'd be livid if it ever happened to my son, but kids being mean to each other usually isn't a criminal offense.

Ultimately, I issued a summons on one count of child abuse to the oldest sister but didn't make a physical arrest. What good would it have done to put this 18-year-old girl in jail? Essentially, I ticketed her, which required her to go to court. She signed the summons, thanked me, and said she was sorry and that she understood she had to stay away from the boys until the courts or Social Services made a determination.

These situations are difficult because many undesirable circumstances don't directly violate the law. Law enforcement relies on Social Services to help improve the undesirable circumstances, but Social Services relies on law enforcement to help build the cases when these circumstances are present. This is why it's important to document everything. Often it isn't clear what's important until later.

This is also why, whenever possible, officers should conduct or help conduct their own interviews. They have firsthand knowledge of the scene, individuals, and circumstances, and their informed insight and diligence can be a huge help in getting critical information down on paper. In this case, the startling contrast in the kids' demeanor at our different meetings led me to ask specific questions that helped me figure out what was going on so that I could give this information to Social Services.

This was a complicated mess, to say the least, and it reveals how law enforcement deals with different shades of grey on a daily basis. Being effective at our jobs requires more than just knowing the written laws. It takes individuals with the patience to truly decipher each situation, an understanding of how the law is meant to be utilized, and the willingness to implement the appropriate action for each situation.

To Err Is Human

Experience is simply the name we give our mistakes.

Oscar Wilde

To err is human, and all law enforcement officials are human. When we are placed in intense and stressful environments that require us to make split-second decisions, the probability of error naturally increases. I say this not to make excuses but rather to give perspective.

I have a speech on my wall by President Theodore Roosevelt that serves as a constant reminder not to lose perspective:

It is not the critic who counts;

not the man who points out how the strong

man stumbles, or where the doer of deeds

101

could have done them better.
The credit belongs to the man
who is actually in the arena, whose face is
marred by dust and sweat and blood; who
strives valiantly; who errs, who comes
short again and again, because there is no
effort without error and shortcoming;
but who does actually strive to do the
deeds; who knows the great enthusiasms,
the great devotions; who spends himself in
a worthy cause; who at the best knows in
the end the triumph of high achievement,
and who at the worst, if he fails, at least
fails while daring greatly, so that his place
shall never be with those cold and timid
souls who know neither victory nor defeat.

When one of our own makes an error, it can be of no consequence, or it can usher in the gravest of repercussions. I have made mistakes, and I hope others can learn from them. One mistake I made involved an officer safety issue that resulted from my failure to conduct a thorough search on the first call I received as an officer.

What a wake-up call it was.

My First Call as Primary Officer

A person who never made a mistake never tried anything.

ALBERT EINSTEIN

One evening, I was dispatched to a disturbance in progress at a two-story single family residence. Upon arrival, I noticed a black SUV with the engine running that had damage to the driver's side and a flat rear tire. The gas lid was open, and the gas cap was sitting on the ground about 10 feet from the vehicle.

The on-duty commander arrived on scene, and the first words out of his mouth were, "Spencer, you really are a shit magnet."

Upon approaching the home, I noticed the splintered doorframe with large pieces of the frame on the floor. I also noticed a hole in the living room wall about the size of a baseball. I verbally contacted the victim inside the home, and she invited me into the house.

The woman was wearing a robe and was visibly upset and scared. She stated that she had been married to the suspect for 10 years, and this was the first time anything like this had ever happened. She stated that they had five kids together ranging in age from 10 months to 10 years old. She stated that the suspect drank regularly and on occasion used marijuana and cocaine. She thought he had drunk at least 12 beers and some whiskey in the past few hours, and she wasn't sure what drugs he might have taken.

I went through the house with her to double check that the kids were okay. They were all in bed and asleep except for the baby, who was wide awake in the crib. We came back downstairs to the kitchen, and she went to check on the puppy in the backyard. She was afraid the suspect had killed it because he was hallucinating and seeing snakes.

She first became aware of his mental state when he came upstairs with a large hunting knife and began stabbing the sheets, saying there were snakes in the bed. She got the knife away from him, but then he grabbed a loaded 9mm semi-automatic handgun from the bedroom that the baby slept in and went downstairs, waving it around.

She was able to get the handgun away from him before he went out the back door and jumped over the fence. She locked the doors, unloaded the handgun, and hid it and the knife upstairs in the bedroom. When she went to the front door to lock it, she noticed their black SUV in the front yard. It was running and had been wrecked.

Then the suspect came around the house and kicked in the front door, splintering the doorframe. He had a car antenna in his hand and was swinging it like a weapon, but he dropped it at the front door. She was on the phone with dispatch at this point and was afraid to tell him she had called 911. Instead, she told him she had called her mother. He went into the kitchen and picked up a large kitchen knife and began swinging it around. He then put the knife on the table.

He told her he wanted his gun so he could kill himself. He started to go upstairs, and she grabbed and pulled on his shirt until it ripped off of him. He then went into the garage and started their car. He backed it into a tree, causing slight damage to the rear of the car.

I asked if she felt afraid, and she stated that she was and that she wasn't going to let him harm her kids. I asked what she thought might have caused his behavior. She said he had gotten mad at her when she hadn't answered his phone call. She stated that she had been bathing the kids at the time. She said this was the first time she had ever threatened to leave him and that might have caused his behavior.

Looking back, there is a very good chance that if she hadn't stopped him from going upstairs, my first call would have been to investigate a murder suicide. I believe this woman prevented the death of her immediate family.

I collected one large hunting knife from the closet in the master bedroom and put it in its scabbard, which was sitting on the floor just outside the closet. I also collected a large kitchen knife from a small table in the kitchen and a 9mm handgun from the top dresser drawer of the master bedroom. This was the handgun the victim had unloaded. I cleared the handgun to confirm that it was unloaded and secured all three items in the front passenger seat of my patrol car.

I was informed that the suspect had driven the black SUV into a neighbor's mailbox and fence; other deputies were covering that case, which had been called in by a neighbor about the same time the wife called in. The neighbor had reported that a man next door was in the front yard stabbing the ground and screaming about snakes. The damage to the vehicle was consistent with the damage caused by a fence and mailbox.

I then spoke with the suspect, who was sitting in the front yard under the supervision of another deputy. The suspect said he had blacked out and didn't remember anything that had happened. He admitted to drinking 12 or so beers and smoking some pot. He also mentioned that this was the first time he'd had one of these episodes or involved his family. He said he thought mushrooms could cause him to black out, but he'd never eaten any. When I asked how he knew that, he said he'd seen it on TV.

I took him into custody and searched him, handcuffed him, placed him in the back of my patrol car, and transported him to the jail complex, but I couldn't administer the Breathalyzer test due to the machine freezing up.

At the jail, during the bookings search, a 9mm bullet was discovered in his front right pocket.

The booking officer gave me a look and handed me the bullet, which had been mixed in with some change. He didn't have to say anything. Although this was a relatively small mistake, I learned the lesson loud and clear. From then on, I thoroughly searched every arrestee I brought in.

Our Mistakes Can Have Lasting Effects

My failures have been errors in judgment, not of intent.

ULYSSES S. GRANT

Mistakes we make that only affect us personally are relatively easy to deal with. When our mistakes affect others, they are more difficult to handle.

When I was assigned to my first death investigation, I didn't know the identity of the deceased. I began my investigation trying to determine who this young man was before the coroner arrived.

The deceased was inside an older motor home. I spoke with the reporting party, and he told me that his friend, the deceased, had been on a three-day drug binge. The last time he knew his friend was alive was between 2:00 and 3:00 a.m. when he heard him snoring. The reporting party woke up around 11:30 a.m. and realized his friend wasn't breathing. He went to the neighbors for help because his phone didn't work, and the neighbor called 911.

The reporting party stated that he didn't know his friend's last name or where he lived; he thought the man was about 30 years old. He stated that the man had shot up meth several times the previous night and had done some LSD and other pills he'd brought with him. The man completed a written statement and gave us written consent to search the motor home.

During the search, I located two used syringes in a red sharps box in a cabinet in the motor home and booked them into evidence. I also found a prescription bottle that didn't belong to the reporting party. I took pictures of the interior of the motor home during my search and booked all 46 pictures into evidence, then assisted the coroner in removing and loading the deceased into the coroner's vehicle.

The vehicle the man had driven to the motor home was registered to a female, and I had dispatch track down an address and phone number. I was so eager to discover the man's identity that I didn't give proper consideration to the possible relationship between the registered owner and the deceased.

While trying to determine the man's identity, I spoke over the phone with an upset mother who had been trying to find her son for several days. Inexperienced and unsure of myself, I didn't know if I could tell her about the deceased at this time, so I kept her in the dark.

In hindsight, this was a mistake. Imagine if your son had been missing for three days and a cop called asking about your vehicle and didn't reveal the condition of your son. As a parent, I can't think of a worse thing a cop could do.

Had I waited for the coroner's arrival before beginning my investigation, I would have known the identity of the deceased because I would have had access to the driver's license in the man's wallet. This incident taught me a very valuable lesson about not proceeding with an investigation without first giving consideration to the people involved. In my zealousness, I made my investigation more important than people, but I learned that in order to do my job better, I needed to consider people first. This lesson has stuck with me ever since.

Mistakes are easier to forgive when people are open, honest, and remorseful, and this is why law enforcement officers need to be transparent about the mistakes we make. That is how we gain and keep the trust of the people we serve. Our society's overuse of civil litigation is the direct enemy of that transparency. We usually have the right intentions, but many people don't want to admit their mistakes for fear of being sued. It would be refreshing if people were judged on the intent of their actions instead of being viewed as an opportunity to profit when mistakes are made.

When We Run Out of Patience

When anger rises, think of the consequences.

CONFUCIUS

Cops are people too. Some things try our patience more than others, and this too can lead to mistakes. At times, especially when small kids were hurt or killed, my emotions became raw, my patience suffered, and I lost my self-control.

On one memorable occasion, I struggled to remain patient while directing traffic for an extended period of time in the aftermath of an accident that was so bad, the highway had been shut down. I'd parked my patrol car sideways, blocking the lanes on the highway with my overhead and strobe lights on. I'd also positioned my vehicle as a barrier between oncoming traffic and myself while directing traffic onto county roads in a detour around the accident, which was a mile down the highway.

I was amazed at how many people drove onto the shoulder, went around my vehicle, and approached me to ask if they could keep going down the highway. Each time, I had to stop the flow of traffic so the driver could back up and go the way I was directing everyone. It's true that many individuals don't know an alternate route or what to do when they can't take their normal route, but these folks sure made my job tougher.

At least one toddler had been killed in this horrific accident, and a few more kids had been injured. Three to four hours into directing traffic, a young lady about 18 to 20 years old blew past me on the shoulder, clearly intending to keep going. I began yelling at her, and she stopped about 100 yards past me. She rolled down her window and said, "What? I thought I could go this way."

I looked back at my patrol car with all its lights flashing, blocking both lanes of traffic, and yelled, "What do you think I'm doing here?"

She started to say something, and I cut her off, yelling, "There are dead people down there, so you need to back up and go where I direct you!"

A look of shock filled her face, and she had difficulty verbalizing an apology as she backed up.

Looking back, I regret treating her in this fashion, but whenever a child was killed, it threw me. It always made me question whether there was any justice in the world, and my patience suffered accordingly. On this occasion and others, what brought me back into perspective was the realization that in spite of our mistakes, we police officers have a profoundly positive impact on society. That kept me going, in spite of it all.

Swearing on the Job

When you reach the end of your rope,
tie a knot in it and hang on.

FRANKLIN D. ROOSEVELT

Let me just come out and admit that most police officers like to swear. For better or for worse, this tension diffuser does an admirable job of keeping us from blowing up at times when our patience is tried to the max. The problem is, sometimes we're pushed to our limits and no longer consider our reservations and professionalism. This is a problem, because the fact is, we are professionals in the public spotlight.

I lost my cool late one Friday afternoon at the end of a long week. It was very hot, close to 100 degrees with no shade, and I'd been assigned to help another deputy with a possible sexual assault. I was on the scene so long I finally needed to turn my vehicle off so it wouldn't run out fuel.

I was getting little to no feedback on the status of the case in spite of repeated attempts to contact my supervisor, but after cooking in my vehicle for hours, I was notified that I could release the scene. At this point, I'd already extended my shift and had multiple hours of reports to complete on my cases for the week.

While en route back to the sheriff's office, a detective notified me that I had another report to complete for this case, even though the case wasn't mine. I was exhausted, frustrated, and annoyed, to say the least.

Over the radio, another deputy asked me when I was going to be done with the vehicle.

I thought was a dumb question. What did it matter to him? I had no idea my car partner had asked him to ask me. Car partners use the same vehicle; they give it to their partner when they're off duty and drive it when they're on duty.

I had no idea when I'd be done with the reports I needed to complete, and besides, I still needed to fuel and clean the vehicle, so I told the deputy I didn't know when I'd be done.

He came back on and said that wasn't good enough, and that's when my frustration got the better of me. At the end of my rope, I snatched up the radio and stated, "You'll get the car when you [insert F-bomb] get it!"

Police channels are monitored open broadcasts and are required to follow certain guidelines. If I'd dropped the F-bomb on the primary station, the sheriff's office could have been fined tens of thousands of dollars. How fortunate that we were only on the tactical channel!

Nonetheless, I was reprimanded for swearing and informed that communications between employees should be professional, especially on the radio, regardless of what channel we were on. I had violated both the code of ethics and the prohibited speech expression and conduct policy in my county, and I received a letter of warning documenting this infraction and informing me that any further violations would result in disciplinary action up to and including termination.

I knew I'd messed up by swearing on a public broadcast. I was always open and honest about my mistakes, in part because I wanted other people to learn from them and not have to make them themselves. I also tried to learn from other people's mistakes. When you're learning and doing, you're going to make mistakes. Cops are learning and doing on a daily basis. The important thing is to learn and improve. Otherwise, we continue to make the same mistakes over and over.

The next day, I was forced to come and face the music for my actions and receive a letter of reprimand.

Later that year, I was awarded Deputy of the Year. Naturally, the running joke became that all you needed

to do to receive this coveted award was drop the F-bomb
on the radio.

How Relationships Pay Off

Peace is not absence of conflict,
it is the ability to handle conflict by peaceful means.

RONALD REAGAN

As a law enforcement officer, I often preferred working alone. My standards were high, and I didn't want sloppy mistakes to compromise an investigation, nor did I want to have to redo work thanks to someone else's less than stellar approach.

That said, I prided myself on working well with everyone, from my fellow law enforcement officers to neighboring agencies to criminals, victims, and witnesses. I knew instinctively that relationships were the key to my success. I also knew that if the people I was there to help couldn't see past my uniform, I wasn't going to get anywhere.

This is why I treated people with respect and didn't judge or speak down to them. In return, I routinely got information and cooperation from criminals and individuals who don't normally cooperate with law enforcement, all because of how I interacted with them.

One Thing Leads to Another

Never in the field of human conflict was so much owed by so many to so few.

Winston S. Churchill

One time, I was dispatched to a felony warrant at a residence. I arrived on scene with two local police officers and knocked on the front door with one of the officers while the other officer went to the back of the residence.

The officer in back communicated via radio that the suspect was running out the back door. We went around the residence and found the suspect on his knees about 50 feet from the trailer.

I handcuffed the individual, identified him as the wanted party, took him over to the back of my patrol car, and searched him. I discovered green baggies in his front left pocket, one of which contained a white residue, and a yellow glass pipe in his right front pocket, along with a wallet and I.D.

While the suspect was on the ground and I was in the process of handcuffing him, he rose up on his hand, scraping his knuckle and making it bleed. I secured the suspect in my patrol car and called for medical to come check him out.

We were contacting other people at the residence when I recognized the name of a young woman as being a wanted party. I contacted clearance, and they confirmed a valid felony warrant for her. I took her into custody and placed her in the back of one of the other police officer's vehicles.

The homeowner of the residence requested I come inside so she could speak with me. She told me that on the previous day, the man I had in custody had assaulted the woman who was in custody. He had placed his left hand over her nose and mouth and punched her in the ribs with his right hand. The homeowner yelled at him and separated them, and the assault had stopped. The homeowner also showed me photos of injuries sustained by the woman over the previous week; these included bruising. The homeowner completed a written statement and said she would email me the photos.

I questioned the woman about the assault, and she denied that it had happened. I questioned the man about the assault, and he too denied anything had happened.

While looking for the woman's I.D. and searching the man's bags, one of the officers uncovered a Crown Royal bag containing a variety of drug paraphernalia including needles, bands to strap the arms with, and small containers. I tested a small container with a brown liquid substance and got negative results, so I booked it as an unknown substance. I completed a test of the white residue in the bag found in this man's front left pocket, and it showed presumptive positive for methamphetamine; I also identified two pills as acetaminophen/oxycodone.

The homeowner noticed that several items in the suitcase belonged to her. She didn't want to press charges for the theft, so that portion of the case was victim failed. The items were returned to the homeowner, who completed a written statement to include witnessing the assault and the items that were stolen.

Another individual on scene came back with a suspended driver's license for lack of payment of child support. I seized his driver's license and completed a proof of service for him.

The homeowner told me that the man and woman in custody had a four-month-old. The baby was believed to be with the woman's mother, who lived in another city. I contacted Social Services about the baby since both parents were in custody, and I also contacted the victim's advocate to check into bond conditions for the man.

Most bond conditions state that the individual cannot violate any laws or city ordinances. In my state, law enforcement isn't able to see bond conditions (this may be in the process of changing), but the victim's advocate does have access to bond conditions. This is why it's so important for the victim's advocate and law enforcement to work together. Otherwise, cases aren't necessarily handled and charged appropriately.

The next day, I received a copy of the man's bond condition. Condition #7 stated, "You may not posses or consume alcohol or marijuana. No controlled substance use except for medication currently prescribed by a physician." Condition #10 stated, "Do not violate any state or federal law or municipal ordinance."

The suspect had knowingly violated both of these conditions. He was charged while in custody with violation of bail bond conditions, which is a class 6 felony.

I had a good rapport with the homeowner thanks to previous experiences at this address in regard to narcotics complaints. Without this rapport, I never would have known about the assault or the theft. I ended up submitting 15 names with over 20 vehicles to the crime analyst and charging the suspect with assault and possession of narcotics and paraphernalia. He also had a felony warrant, and the next day, I added the additional felony charge of violating his bond condition.

We Have Clowns

The world is a dangerous place to live;
not because of the people who are evil,

but because of the people who don't do anything about it.

ALBERT EINSTEIN

My professionalism and thoroughness also paid dividends when a case opened up in which the reporting party was an individual I'd worked with on a prior case.

I was dispatched to a reported cold burglary at a residence. The reporting party was the grown son of the property owners, and the suspect was his sister's kid. With his parents out of town for a month, the reporting party had been checking on the house when he'd noticed a broken window on an attached back porch but no sign of forced entry to the house itself.

I collected and booked numerous drugs and drug paraphernalia into evidence after finding many types and quantities of pills in a plastic bag on the bar upstairs along with a prepared syringe filled with a clear liquid.

In the basement, I found glove tips, which are routinely used to store drugs.

The primary suspect was the grandson of the home-owner. He was reported to be a Juggalo, a member of a gang that dresses up as clowns. He was also a heavy drug user who lived on the street.

I spoke to the homeowners by phone while they were away, and they advised me of a theft that had occurred several weeks earlier. A Beretta .25 handgun had been stolen as well as a moneybag containing $5,000.00. That large sum of cash had been intended to fund their vacation.

Two weeks later, the reporting party called in a second time to report a burglary in progress by the same suspect.

While en route, I requested additional units. Given that a handgun had been stolen and that we were dealing with the same suspects, it was likely they'd be armed. I then requested the radio channel be cleared and dedicated to the call.

While approaching the residence, I saw the reporting party standing in the middle of the road. He told me he'd detained the primary suspect at the residence and waved me in the direction the suspect vehicle had fled.

I pulled over the Jeep Cherokee about one half mile from the residence.

As soon as the vehicle stopped, both the driver and passenger immediately displayed their hands out of the windows, something that's distinctly unusual to see. I ordered the driver to turn off the vehicle, and he complied. Another police officer arrived on scene, putting his vehicle next to mine. The reporting party on scene had detained the third suspect, so I directed additional responding units to the residence.

I came up to the passenger side of the vehicle, opened the door, and directed the passenger back to the police officers on scene. When the passenger got out of the seat, I saw a package of razor blades and numerous other drug paraphernalia sitting there along with a camouflaged backpack on the floorboard. The bag was open with a firearm inside. The police officer was still searching both parties, and I announced I'd found a gun. Simultaneously, the police officer's search revealed a pair of metal knuckles and a clear baggie in the passenger's front pocket.

I removed the magazine from the Beretta .25 handgun, which was loaded, and opened the breach of the firearm, which was empty.

The driver and passenger were placed in separate patrol cars, and a police officer and I searched the vehicle. We found numerous items including syringes, containers, baggies, pipes, marijuana, a scale, pills, a prescription morphine container with residue prescribed to someone else, straws, aluminum foil, spoons (for cooking and cutting), steel wool, a CO2 container, a pill cutter, the medication lidocaine, and razor blades. Other items included the handgun, .22 ammunition, 10-gauge ammunition, .38 ammunition, a box for .25 caliber ammunition, knives, cell phones, a car stereo, and multiple holsters (none of them fit the Beretta). In all, the stuff covered four large tables we put together.

Another deputy arrived at the residence and took custody of the third and primary suspect. He was wearing a holster containing a new .40 Glock and showed signs of being under the influence of drugs. He also had a backpack with clothes, drug paraphernalia, drugs, and a zip lock bag of change.

I interviewed the driver of the vehicle after he signed a Miranda advisement. He stated that he'd just met up with the other two that day and didn't know what was going on. He said he didn't have a valid driver's license and wasn't a drug user.

I interviewed the primary suspect after he signed a Miranda advisement. He said he didn't know anything about the Beretta .25 except that it belonged to the passenger. He stated that he'd entered the residence earlier that day to get some of his clothing. He told another deputy he was high at the time. He stated that he knew he wasn't supposed to be there.

I asked him about going into the residence two weeks earlier, and he again stated that he knew he wasn't supposed to be in the residence but had gone there to sleep.

I interviewed the passenger after he signed a Miranda advisement. He stated that he hadn't gone into the residence, although he'd gone on to the property, and I asked him about going into the residence two weeks earlier. He said he'd been told they could be there by the primary suspect, but while they were there, a woman – the primary suspect's aunt – had advised him that they weren't allowed to be in the house or on the property.

I asked him about the Beretta, and he said it was the primary suspect's. I asked who owned the camouflaged backpack, and he said it was his. I asked him why the Beretta was in his backpack, and he didn't answer. I asked who the morphine had been prescribed to. He stated it belonged to his dead grandfather. I asked him about the prescription morphine container, and he said he'd stolen it from his grandparent's house. He also stated that the marijuana and digital scale were his, as were some of the syringes and two of the rigs he used to shoot up with. He also stated that they'd entered the residence today to get some gas money. He was almost out of gas, and the primary suspect had promised him some gas money.

I spoke with the owners by phone a second time and asked where they kept their loose change. I needed to prove that the crime of burglary had also been committed. The primary suspect had in his possession a bag of change, and this required me to confirm that the homeowners had kept change in the residence.

They stated they had a bank in the bedroom. I located the bank and found it empty, but previously, one of the homeowners' daughters had checked the property and observed the change in the jar. This was important, because it added an additional crime of burglary with the primary suspect being armed with a handgun while committing the crime, which is an enhancer.

The driver was cited for the driving offense and arrested on an active warrant, and the passenger was arrested on an active warrant. The passenger was additionally charged with possession of drugs, possession of a dangerous weapon (metal knuckles), theft (possessing the .25 handgun), possession of drug paraphernalia, and one count of trespassing.

The primary suspect was charged with theft (of the cash and the .25 Beretta), trespassing on the first incident, burglary while armed on the second incident (the bag of change), prohibited use of a weapon (possessing a weapon while under the influence of drugs), possession of drugs, and possession of drug paraphernalia.

I met with the homeowner after he returned from vacation. Sure enough, he confirmed that his locking bank bag containing $5,000.00 was missing. Also missing was a black Beretta .25, a black biker's wallet with chain, the change, and some prescription medication.

The homeowner also noted that a full piggy bank of change, a box of gloves, and an in-dash stereo/cd player were missing from inside his shop building, a garage detached from the residence. The items had been stolen a month earlier when the suspect had been caught trespassing in the residence by the victim's daughter. The south garage door had been damaged a month earlier and was the method of entry into the shop building.

A small locking safe was located in a room where the primary suspect kept some of his belongings. When the safe was opened, we found the grandfather's wallet with all of his identification cards and credit cards. I photographed the wallet and contents and returned them to the rightful owner.

The safe also contained five syringes, one spoon, two burnt straws, two lighters, and prescription medication.

With the new items and information, I requested that the DA modify the existing charges and add new ones. This investigation consisted of three to four cases rolled into one, depending on how you looked at it. In short, it was extremely complicated and very involved, just the kind of case I had the knack for attracting.

All the parties helped me, including the suspects, because they admitted almost every one of their crimes. Because I educated the homeowner's grown children, they were observant about things like the loose change and when it was and was not on scene. The reporting party spoke to me numerous times about the suspects and informed me whenever he checked on the property. He did all of this because he cared about his parents but he also went the extra mile with me because I went the extra mile with him in dealing with his sibling and nephew.

A few days after closing this case, a seasoned veteran deputy who assisted me told me that its complexity and the sheer amount of evidence we'd collected had mentally exhausted him. I was used to these types of cases, so yes, I was tired, but I was better prepared mentally than most because of my constant exposure to complicated cases.

Teamwork

Competition has been shown to be useful up to a certain point and no further, but cooperation, which is the thing we must strive for today, begins where competition leaves off.

FRANKLIN D. ROOSEVELT

I was in the habit of turning on my radio while driving to the station to pick up my patrol car. This helped me focus mentally and prepare for my upcoming shift.

One morning, a call came in about a fire that had originated at a front door. Fires don't start at front doors by themselves, so I took notice of the address and possible people involved.

Meanwhile, I was dispatched to a call about a stolen vehicle at a residence. I arrived on scene and spoke with the homeowner, who stated that his 2011 Chevy Silverado had been stolen during the night, sometime between 9:00 p.m. and 8:00 a.m.

In the east ditch on the county road in front of the residence was a crashed Honda Sedan with an obscured temporary tag in the back window covered by snow. I had clearance run the vehicle identification number, and it came back as belonging to the primary suspect in the arson case.

I contacted the police department and also notified my commander, who immediately requested the on-call field evidence technician, or FET, be dispatched to my location.

The owner of the stolen truck told me his vehicle had the security and safety system called OnStar. I spoke with OnStar's representative, who advised me that the stolen pickup was now in another county. I requested that sheriff's office sit on the vehicle until I arrived.

While waiting for support to arrive on the initial scene, I learned from the police officer in charge of the arson investigation of multiple associations who might be involved with the suspect, including a woman who had the same last name as the suspect and another man.

I messaged the dispatch center to query the Department of Motor Vehicles database, and they were able to locate the dates of birth of both individuals along with an address outside the county. I secured the scene until the FET and commander arrived on scene.

The commander walked up, asking, "Why is it always you, Spencer?" Sure enough, we were embarking on another incredibly complicated case.

I showed the FET the shoe impressions that led to the house and where I'd walked around the vehicle. I had the police department's case linked with mine, and the police officer requested we secure the vehicle; he then had the vehicle towed and impounded.

I drove to the location of the stolen truck. Because it was in a different county and jurisdiction, I worked side by side with a deputy who led me to various locations throughout the day.

The deputy secured the vehicle and scene while her sergeant and I followed the shoe impressions through a trail south of the vehicle and then back east. We followed the shoe impressions for approximately a quarter mile until they disappeared in front of a residence.

I spoke with the homeowner of the residence, who advised us that between 4:00 and 6:00 a.m., his barking dogs had awakened him. This timeframe was consistent with the crimes, since the arson call had occurred at 4:00 in the morning.

I stayed on the scene and went over some research with the other deputy until support arrived. The deputy and I spoke with an individual on location, who advised us that the mother of one of the parties of interest lived nearby.

At both scenes, we observed impressions of Air Jordan shoes in the snow leading up to and away from the stolen vehicle. The deputy and I went to the address we'd been given and found similar shoe impressions in the snow leading up to the doorstep.

I knocked on the door and was greeted by the party of interest's mother, who stated that we had just missed him and that he was working in town. I referenced the shoes on the front steps, and it was unclear who they belonged to. The mother stated that her son and his daughter had recently moved back in with her. I briefly explained the situation, and she consented to a search of her residence. The deputy and I searched the residence but did not find the suspect.

The FET came to my location to photograph the shoe impressions and collect the shoes, and soon after, we received information from the sergeant that he had located the party of interest at a job site. The deputy and I went to that location and spoke with the suspect. He was unfamiliar with the shoes on the front step and completed a written statement.

About that time, I received information from the field evidence technician that the shoes didn't match the impressions left on scene by the suspect. The deputy and I went to the next lead at another residence in another city. We spoke with the renter, who said the female party of interest and the suspect had been kicked out approximately four months earlier.

A third police department was requested to track down a lead in their jurisdiction but came up negative.

Then I received a phone call from a police officer stating that he had a lead on an individual who had been called to pick up the suspect early this morning in the town where the stolen truck was located. The individual's address was only a few miles from our current location. I asked the deputy if she knew the individual and his address.

She said, "Oh yeah, we deal with him all the time, but he won't tell you anything."

I said, "Well, let's just go and talk to him."

The individual came to the door and spoke with us outside. He was very defensive and didn't want to speak with us. I asked if we could go inside to talk, since I'd been outside most of the day and it was cold. He agreed, and as we walked into the home, I noticed a flat screen TV lying face down on the dining room table with the back panel removed.

In a friendly voice, I asked what he was doing with the TV, and he told me that he took the broken flat screens, replaced an inexpensive component, and resold them for a good profit. I said, "Wow, that is really smart. I wouldn't know how to do that." This interaction leveled the playing field and made us equals, just two individuals doing our jobs. Then I asked him what had happened that morning, and he told me step by step what had transpired.

Out of the blue, he suddenly stated, "You know what, I can do better than that. I can try to get a location for you." He took out his cell phone and texted the suspect, attempting to get his current location. The suspect never replied, but it was an amazing breakthrough for a career criminal to offer to assist me in a fashion I hadn't even requested.

I glanced over at the other deputy while the individual was texting the suspect, and she looked at me like I had two heads or something.

The individual completed a written statement that he'd picked up and dropped off the suspect at a fairly close location in the city shortly before 6:00 a.m. after the suspect had directed him in what he described as an "unfamiliar pattern." He said the suspect claimed people were chasing him and had admitted he was "whacked out his mind."

The individual stated that the suspect was wearing a long-sleeved black shirt or jacket with blue jeans and shoes and that he had a large black dog on a leash.

I put the word out to the surrounding areas, with special attention to the city, and then got a call from the police officer stating that he'd received an update from the suspect's mother that the suspect had a storage unit in another city he was reported to have lived out of.

The officer contacted the police department in the city where the storage unit was located. After doing some checking, they informed the officer that the suspect and a female had been at the location approximately an hour earlier in a U-Haul truck.

The officer contacted U-Haul directly and found the truck had been rented from a location in the city I was in.

I notified dispatch with this update, and the deputy and I went to the U-Haul rental location. When we pulled into the parking lot, on our right was a 14-foot U-Haul truck with a female in the passenger seat and a white male standing in front of the vehicle talking on a phone.

I recognized the individual from looking at a booking photo. I made contact with both him and the female passenger, who identified herself as the party of interest. I took the suspect into custody to do an interview for the two active investigations.

The company that rented the U-Haul advised me that the suspect had not completed returning the U-Haul and needed to check it in. I allowed this, and the company gave me the receipt of the contract. I kept a copy and put a copy in the suspect's property since he owed a balance to U-Haul for the rental.

A deputy from the other county transported the female passenger to the station for voluntary questioning and a written statement. She stated that she and the suspect had gotten into a fight the night before and that the suspect had picked her up at 9:00 in the morning in the U-Haul truck. The suspect had briefly mentioned that his car was stuck in a ditch somewhere but had been vague about the details. Early that afternoon, she'd become aware of the arson incident at the suspect's mother's house. That portion of the city where the house was located was in another county.

My on-duty commander asked if I wanted him to call in a detective to interview the suspect, but I told him no, that I believed the suspect wanted to speak with me.

The suspect completed and signed a Miranda advisement stating that he understood his rights and wanted to speak with me without a lawyer present. I then recorded an interview with him via digital recorder. In the interview, he admitted to multiple crimes, including attempted murder, arson, trespassing, stealing a vehicle, and failure to report an accident. He said he wanted to kill his mother because he believed the Hell's Angels biker gang had killed her, surgically removed her face, and put it on this other woman who was pretending to be his mother.

I arrested the suspect on the stolen vehicle charge, the felony trespass, and the failure to report an accident that had occurred in the county and transported him to jail. I advised booking that the suspect had made a suicidal statement about wanting to pour gasoline on himself and light himself on fire. I collected all the suspect's clothes except for his hat and boxers and booked them into evidence for the police department's arson case because his clothes would have absorbed vapors from the gasoline while he was making the fire bombs he'd used to set fire to his mother's front door.

I also booked into evidence a hammer, pocketknife, and an extra pair of shoes similar to the impressions left at the first two scenes. I took photographs of all the items and booked them into evidence as well.

I then forwarded this case to the police department. In my affidavit, I included the charges that would be filed in the adjacent county of attempted first-degree murder and first-degree arson so the judge would be aware of them when the suspect attended his bond hearing.

After this case was complete and I took a step back, I was in awe of what had transpired. You can go your entire career without catching an attempted homicide suspect, much less have the opportunity to coordinate the actions of other supporting agencies. This was an excellent example of multiple law enforcement agencies working together. If even one of the agencies hadn't been able to assist in the fashion they did, it's quite possible we wouldn't have apprehended the suspect.

In all, five separate agencies were involved. I had the unique privilege of coordinating the entire case with one other officer, and I was truly grateful for all the assistance from my neighboring agencies.

I will never be able to express the full impact this experience had on me. Sometimes call loads don't allow us to help each other much, but this is a shining example of what can be achieved when we all work together and of how we can get career criminals to assist us if we handle ourselves – and them – properly.

Beyond the Call of Duty

Sometimes when I consider what tremendous consequences
come from little things..
I am tempted to think...there are no little things.

BRUCE BARTON

At the beginning of each week, I went through the calls that had come in on my days off, searching for new active warrants in or near my district. I kept a binder on active warrants in my area, and I routinely pulled photos of the wanted parties and added them to my binder. When I had down time, I tracked down these wanted parties.

I also approached warrants differently than most of my fellow deputies did. Some would open a warrant call and then just knock on a door. When no one answered, they would clear the call and consider their work done.

I treated each warrant like an investigation, visiting numerous locations to speak with neighbors, employers, leasing offices, schools, and so on in an attempt to determine if the wanted individual was still in the area and, if so, where.

Schools were often involved. One time, after the FBI called the school, I got a lead from a school resource officer that a person with a federal warrant was in the area and that her kids had just registered at the school. I followed the information and ended up catching the individual at a rural residence.

It usually takes only five to 10 minutes to get a confirmation of a warrant out of your jurisdiction, but this particular federal warrant took close to 30 minutes, since it involved the FBI and Drug Enforcement Agency. Needless to say, most officers go their entire careers without catching someone with a federal warrant.

I always held myself to a higher standard than was required, but I never took work home, and I kept my work life separate from my personal life. Back when I played ice hockey, I had the ability to compartmentalize things. From the moment I put the gear on until I took it off, nothing mattered except the game and my performance.

The same went for my uniform as a law enforcement officer. Once I put it on, nothing else mattered except the call and my performance. When I was on duty and something at home needed to be taken care, whether it was a decision to make, a bill to pay, or an event to schedule or attend, my wife took care of it.

My focus on details also benefited me. The vast majority of my cases were pleaded, which meant I seldom went to court. In spite of all my cases, I only went to court three or four times, and only one of those was on a day off.

Our schedule was five 10-hour days on followed by four to five days off, depending on our training cycle. I used every bit of my time off to enjoy my family and hobbies and to recharge my batteries for the next time I put on the uniform.

Overall, I credit my wife with my ability to do my job. I cannot overstate the importance she played. When I was at work, she wanted all my attention on what I was doing. She never wanted me to be distracted from the task at hand because I might miss something that could endanger fellow deputies or myself.

When I was home, I was fully at home, and when I was on the job, I was fully on the job. I hated unsolved cases, and I left no stone unturned in my goal to solve them, as the following experience reveals.

Following Instincts

Our greatest weakness lies in giving up.
The most certain way to succeed is always to try
just one more time.

THOMAS A. EDISON

I was dispatched to a call about a vehicle that had been stolen from a farm. The reporting party told me someone had taken his Honda Accord, driven it to the end of the driveway, and gotten it stuck. Then the suspect had entered the detached garage and stolen the caller's grandmother's 2006 Chevy Impala, leaving a 2000 Nissan Frontier on the property.

I located a shoe impression at the front driver's side in the dirt, where the vehicle was stuck, and I processed the Honda for DNA evidence as well.

I requested the neighboring sheriff's office contact the registered owner of the Nissan Frontier, and this turned up an address only a few miles away in the neighboring county. Two deputies responded to the registered owner's address and spoke to a person on the property who stated the owner was away on a fishing trip; this individual wasn't aware the truck was missing.

Both deputies and the relative of the registered owner of the Nissan responded to my location. I processed the

Nissan for DNA but wasn't able to get any prints from the outside driver's side door. The relative stated that two wet black socks in the bed of the truck, a wet white t-shirt in the cab, and a wet cell phone did not belong to the truck.

There was a considerable amount of mud inside the vehicle. I collected the sock, shirt, and cell phone. The relative backed up the Nissan, and I photographed the shoe impression, which was similar to the shoe impression left near the Honda.

I released the Nissan to the relative, who told me a single black key was missing from the ignition. I also released the Honda back to its owner. Meanwhile, another deputy got a suspicious vehicle call about a 2000 Ford F350 pickup truck sitting in a cornfield; it was registered to a woman who lived a few miles from the cornfield.

I met with the deputy and the registered owner of the Ford at her residence. She stated that she was unaware her truck was missing. When we checked out the vehicle in the cornfield, the only thing missing was the key fob.

The woman then noticed a vehicle that did not belong to her on the back of her property, a 2006 Chevy Impala with in-state plates. This was the vehicle that had been stolen from the garage. The keys were still in the ignition. No damage had been done to the vehicle, and a little bit of mud was on the floor mat.

A neighbor stated that he'd seen a Hispanic male with a slender build in a cream-colored long-sleeved shirt and tan pants in the truck, driving eastbound. I drove east on the county road and observed a middle-aged male sitting in a ravine, in an open space, approximately 100 yards south of the road.

I contacted the man, and he matched the description I'd just been given. I asked how he'd gotten there, and he stated that he'd left his white truck in a cornfield just up the road – this was where we'd recovered the stolen F350 pickup truck.

At the back of the property, we spoke to a homeowner on the north side of the fence. He'd seen the male sleeping in the ditch and thought he was dead. He'd yelled at him and awakened him, but since he wasn't bothering anyone, the homeowner had given him some food and water and let him go about his business. The homeowner had then continued to shoot at prairie dogs on his property while the man sat in the ravine.

I placed the suspect under arrest and searched him. In his front right pocket was a keychain with a Ford key and key fob. I noticed that he was barefoot inside his shoes. He had a lot of mud all over his clothes, and they were still wet.

The other deputy returned the truck keys after starting the vehicle to confirm they were the right keys. I also found a single black key inside the suspect's wallet that fit the description of the Nissan key. I read the suspect his Miranda rights, and he chose to remain silent. I transported him to the county jail and completed two bonding sheets with a total of eight different felony charges.

It's important to be familiar with the agricultural laws in your jurisdiction. In my state, trespassing on agricultural property becomes a felony if the intent is to commit a separate felony. I needed to determine that the property was actually zoned agricultural, which I did by contacting the county clerk and recorders office. During the booking process, when the corrections officer removed the man's shoes, I collected them for evidence. Upon examination, I determined they were similar to the impressions discovered around the vehicles.

I photographed all the vehicles and scenes, processed all the vehicles for prints and DNA, and booked all the DNA evidence before returning the vehicles to their owners. I also took DNA samples from the owners of the vehicles as well as people who were known to drive the vehicles and booked them into evidence in order to obtain a clearer DNA profile of the suspect.

I'm often asked what contributed to my success in law enforcement. Sticking with the job and taking care of the details was a big part of it. A lot of people would have stopped investigating the area before locating the suspect in order to book evidence and write the report, given how many hours of clerical work were involved based on the number of vehicles that had been stolen.

There would have been nothing wrong with this decision, particularly since I only had about two hours left in my shift, but I went with my instinct and continued to search the area. I knew the suspect was headed east and that he was on foot, most likely looking for another vehicle. The extra time I put in paid off, and I was able to arrest the suspect and eventually close the case. Making the arrest added several more hours of work, turning a 10-hour day into close to a 17-hour day, but I never let the amount of time needed to do the job factor in.

Thankfully, my supervisor always authorized the overtime I needed to do the job to the best of my ability. I liked the closure and sense of completion I felt when I finished a case. In this instance, had I not found and arrested the suspect, the case likely would have been suspended. DNA evidence isn't processed in property crimes unless the suspect is known. I went beyond the call of duty, but as far as I'm concerned, it's my duty to go beyond the call of duty. My work simply couldn't always end when my shift ended, nor could I keep from helping in every way I could when tragedies occurred.

What If This Had Been My Family?

Life's most persistent and urgent question is,
"What are you doing for others?"

MARTIN LUTHER KING JR.

Accidents occur every day. Some are a nuisance and take up your time, while others permanently alter your life.

I've responded to a lot of accidents, and I can confidently say that properly fastened seat belts and child restraints are very effective in saving lives and minimizing injuries. Excessive speed is usually a contributing factor in most injuries and fatal accidents, and most accidents occur because the driver is distracted or impaired. If everyone wore a seat belt, slowed down, and focused on driving, the accident rate would plummet.

One particular accident caused by an exhausted driver deeply impacted me. As always, I did my best to go beyond the basic requirements.

Two vehicles were involved, and the sleep-deprived driver was dead. After taking pictures of the scene and vehicles and completing a rough drawing of the resting positions of the vehicles, I headed to the hospital to speak to the driver who had survived the accident. After returning to the accident scene, I gave a written statement and completed a variety of paperwork with the deputy who was the primary on the case, then left.

While I was pulling away, an adult female standing in the road waved me down. After identifying herself, she started asking questions about the vehicles involved in the accident, and I told her to let me pull my car off the road. I parked on the eastbound shoulder and got out. She asked me about her husband, and I told her he had died in the car crash.

Before I was able to say I was sorry, she collapsed. I caught and held her and helped her to the back of my car. I opened the back door and she sat down in the vehicle with her legs outside. I handed her some tissues and knelt in front of her, holding her hands, before requesting dispatch to send a victim's advocate.

She told me her daughters were in her car, parked on a county road nearby, and that they were four and six years old. She gave me her mother's name and number, and I called the woman and explained the situation. The mother stated she was on her way.

When the victim's advocate arrived, she spoke with the woman and went across the street to check on her daughters.

I told the woman I'd arrived on scene less than three minutes after the call came out, and I assured her that her husband didn't suffer. I told her she needed to focus her attention on her two wonderful children.

I spent 20 to 30 minutes with her, and when she was ready, I took two stuffed teddy bears out of my trunk to give to her daughters and walked with her back to her vehicle.

Her parents arrived about 15 minutes later and helped transfer their granddaughters' car seats to their vehicle. The woman completed a consent to search form on her husband's vehicle, locked her vehicle, and left with her kids in her parents' vehicle.

I returned to the accident scene, gave the primary deputy the consent to search form, and left once again, but I couldn't stop thinking about this accident. The woman and her husband were about my age; their children were only a few years older than my son. The husband worked the night shift on an oil and gas rig. He had stayed up to spend Christmas day with his wife and kids and then worked all night. On his way home, he'd fallen asleep at the wheel and drifted into oncoming traffic.

I can still see this woman's face, and I still get emotional when I drive past the scene of the accident. What if my wife had been in her shoes? What if my son had been the child in the car? How would I have wanted the law enforcement officer to treat my family? These questions drive my behavior.

Nabbing a Most Wanted Criminal

It always seems impossible until it is done.

Nelson Mandela

Sometimes, doing my job to the best of my ability meant persevering when others might have called it a day. In one instance, carefully working through the details of what started as a routine traffic stop led to the arrest of a most wanted criminal.

I was attempting to serve a warrant at an apartment building. In the parking lot, I noticed a suspicious vehicle with four individuals inside. The individual I was looking for wasn't present, but while I was returning to my vehicle, the suspicious vehicle pulled out of the parking lot.

I conducted a traffic stop based on the driver's vision being obstructed by a handicap placard, and the vehicle promptly pulled over to the right side of the road. Besides the female driver, there was a male passenger in the front seat and two females in the back. The interior of the vehicle was very messy.

I asked the driver for her license, registration, and proof of insurance. She handed me the registration and proof of insurance and identified herself by name and date of birth but told me she didn't have a license because it was revoked. The front seat passenger didn't have a license either but identified himself by name and date of birth. Previous booking photos confirmed both the driver's and front seat passenger's identities.

I asked how old the passengers in the back were and if they had licenses. One said she was 19 and didn't have a license. The other said she was 23 and that she didn't have a license, either.

I told them someone with a license needed to drive the vehicle or I would need to have it towed. The driver immediately called her mother, who was the registered owner of the vehicle. Meanwhile, I had dispatch run the driver, and she came back with an active warrant and several protection orders. One was an old protection order out of state with her listed as the protected party.

I had dispatch run the male passenger, and he came back with a protection order with the registered owner being the protected party. This was not a no-contact protection order, so it wasn't a problem for the mother to come to the location. Things were getting complicated, so I asked dispatch to locate a second unit, and another deputy soon arrived on scene.

When the registered owner arrived, she gave me permission to search the vehicle.

The driver said she didn't know who the passengers in the back seat were or how old they were. I took her into custody and put her in the back seat of my patrol car for her active warrant.

I told the male passenger he was free to go, and he left a few minutes later on foot.

Meanwhile, I was concerned that the females in the back seat might be juveniles, since they both looked young. The other deputy asked the back seat passenger on the driver's side her name and date of birth. She told him a name and again said she was 19; this information came back clear with no criminal record. This passenger also left the scene on foot.

I asked the remaining passenger her name and date of birth. She was holding a cell phone, and she told me that she was pleading the Fifth Amendment. I told her I was concerned for her safety since I thought she was a juvenile. She told me a name and gave a date of birth that would make her 20 years old. I found this interesting since she had originally told me she was 23. I had dispatch run the name and date of birth, and it came back with no record. I asked how she could possibly not have any record at all, and she stated that she was homeless and only had $2.00. She said her parents had abandoned her and she didn't know where they were. She said she had never gotten a driver's license or an identification card because she didn't have the $12.00 for the Department of Motor Vehicles. She stated that she just went from couch to couch sleeping at random people's houses.

I asked how she could get a cell phone without any identification, and she said the phone belonged to a friend. I asked for the friend's name, but she wouldn't give it to me. I asked how she knew the people in the car, and she said she didn't know them.

This further increased my concern because now I feared she was an at-risk juvenile.

I asked if she knew anyone who could identify her and pick her up, and she said she had an aunt who could pick her up.

She was continually texting or talking on her phone to someone while I spoke to her, and soon she told me she had talked to her aunt, who was on her way.

We had been on scene a while in this residential area, and the neighbors were getting curious. One neighbor in particular caught my attention. She was sitting on the steps around the corner talking on a cell phone. Everyone else was openly watching what we were doing, but she kept looking over her shoulder at us.

I was talking to the other deputy when I overheard the passenger in the back seat say something to the effect of, "I gave them my sister's information."

I confronted her on this statement, and she said she wasn't going to dog out her sister because she had an outstanding warrant. I asked her to step out of the vehicle so we could search it. I asked if anything in the vehicle belonged to her, and she said only the cell phone. She sat on the curb while we conducted the search.

Halfway through our search, I asked if I could call her aunt to get an estimated time she would arrive. She gave us a disconnected phone number and said her aunt would be here soon. I asked if she'd given her aunt the address. She looked around, obviously unaware of our location, which further highlighted her deceit.

The other deputy found an in-state instruction permit to drive in a purse in the back seat. The picture on the ID looked like the passenger and matched her physical description. I had dispatch run it, and it came back with two confirmed felony warrants. Turns out, the girl lying to me and telling me this long, drawn-out sob story was a most wanted criminal.

I confronted her, and she said the permit was her sister's. Of course, I didn't believe her. She had given me information that didn't come back with anything, her age had changed, and the number for her aunt was wrong. In addition, the story that the aunt was coming was false because the girl didn't know where we were. I have to admit, it's true that most criminals lie to us most of the time. This is probably why most cops are decent poker players.

I told the girl to stand up and informed her that she was under arrest for the active warrants and the drug paraphernalia in her purse. She stood up crying and said she was going to jail for what her sister had done, but she was lying about her sister. If she had given me her sister's real date of birth, I would have charged her with identity theft on top of everything else.

When I told her to stand up, the woman sitting on the steps stood up and ran over crying out the suspect's name, the same name that was on the ID.

I told the woman to get back and asked who she was.

She told me she was the suspect's mother.

I asked the woman if she had an ID on her, and she stated that she did not.

The other deputy placed the suspect in the back of his patrol car because I already had the driver in the back of my car.

We completed the search of the vehicle and recovered about a dozen needles, two lighters, several used aluminum foil bundles, a spoon, an IV starter kit, and a small bag with white residue in it. One needle was found under the driver's seat, and another needle was found in the back pocket of the driver's seat with a used foil bundle.

I went over to the patrol car and asked the suspect if she wanted me to explain what was going on to her mother. She said, "Yes, and I have a baggie of drugs in my bra. I don't want to get in trouble for it."

The other deputy and I began transporting both suspects – the driver and the passenger from the back seat – to the jail complex. The passenger's admission was confirmed when she was searched while being booked in the jail complex and a small baggie was discovered in her back left pocket. The other deputy informed us that she'd told him the drug in the small baggie was meth.

As it turns out, the male passenger was on probation and couldn't use or be around drugs or alcohol, but in my state, law enforcement officers can't enforce parole violations. I left a message for his parole officer and forwarded the report to probations.

I arrested the driver on her warrant and charged her with driving with a suspended license. I arrested the passenger on her various warrants, including her most wanted status, and she also received new felony charges.

This was a complicated traffic stop, to say the least. It was also a lengthy traffic stop. Before we knew the identity of the most wanted, the other deputy and my supervisor thought I should let the passenger leave, but I'd explained that I was detaining her because I was concerned for her safety. After I told them her story about being abandoned and homeless and without any money, they were in agreement with me. It was all BS, of course, but that was my justification for holding her.

Carefully working through the details of this case led to the arrest of a most wanted criminal. If I'd been more careful, I might have been able to discover the true identity of the other female passenger as well.

This case had special significance to me for several reasons. For starters, you can go your entire career without catching a most wanted criminal. This fact alone put me on cloud nine. Furthermore, it gave me validation that I could do the job and do it well. I could articulate the reasons for my actions, and my command staff would listen to and agree with me. It was also nice that when I returned to the sheriff's office, the deputy bureau chiefs stopped what they were doing and congratulated me. Some even applauded.

My initial interactions with the most wanted individual were very negative. She would barely speak to me, but I allowed her to keep her cell phone and even speak on it while I proceeded with my investigation. Allowing her to converse with the person on the phone allowed me to gain insight into what was really going on. After I had enough information to call her out on her lies, she became fully cooperative and apologetic. In fact, as soon as I told her she was under arrest, she said, "You just caught a most wanted." The next thing she said was that she had drugs in her bra.

Two weeks later, I spotted the woman driver again driving the same vehicle. She'd been arrested but was out on bail. She saw me turn around and immediately pulled off to the right side of the road next to the curb. She and the same male from the previous stop immediately got out of the vehicle and began approaching my patrol car.

I stepped out of my car and instructed them to get back into the vehicle, and they complied with my instructions.

I approached the driver's side and asked the woman if she'd gotten her license yet. She stated that she had not. She stated that they'd stopped before I'd pulled them over, and then she asked why I'd pulled her over.

I told her I remembered arresting her from the previous incident. Testing me, she asked what her name was. I didn't hesitate and stated her first name. She replied, "Oh, damn."

The fact that I remembered her name made the woman very cooperative, which is why I always tried to address people by name. They played fewer games.

I contacted the owner of the vehicle by phone, and she gave me consent to search the vehicle.

Another deputy read both individuals their Miranda rights, and they both stated that they understood their rights and would continue to speak with me. The woman even stated that she could recite her Miranda rights from memory and that she knew them better than she knew the Pledge of Allegiance.

During the search of the vehicle, I discovered seven used syringes, numerous types of pills, two large spoons with black coating on the bottom, and other drug paraphernalia. I also located numerous prescription drugs (one was a schedule IV) in the vehicle that had not been prescribed to either individual.

The woman admitted that the prescription drugs weren't hers, and the man admitted that the syringes and drug paraphernalia were his. He admitted that he was shooting and smoking oxycodone. He stated that he'd last used oxycodone, a schedule II controlled substance, two days earlier. He stated that he'd gotten it from the woman's mom.

I charged and arrested the man for possession of a schedule II controlled substance. I charged and arrested the woman for driving without a license and possession of a schedule IV controlled substance.

On the way to jail, I asked the man about the female in the back seat on the driver's side the last time I'd encountered them. He told me her name and date of birth and said she'd lied to us that day because she had an active warrant. She came back clear because she'd given me someone else's name and date of birth. I wrote a felony warrant for her for giving the false information, and she was arrested at a later date on that warrant.

It's clear to see that how I treated these individuals on a prior incident paid off when I encountered them a second time. Both parties were extremely cooperative, and the male assisted me in solving another portion of the case that ultimately resulted in another felony arrest.

How we are required to respond today is a direct result of how we proceeded yesterday. We need to consistently get better results the right way, right away. When we accomplish this, we provide justice to the people we serve.

Why should law enforcement go beyond the call of duty?

Because what we do out there truly matters.

Tools in the Toolbox

Education is the most powerful weapon
which you can use to change the world.

NELSON MANDELA

I paid attention, worked hard, and didn't cut corners, but the thing that made me so successful was my ability to get help, and not where you might think.

I'm referring to getting my dispatchers, victim's advocates, victims, suspects, and their friends and families – in other words, non-law enforcement personnel in general – to help me.

I'm also referring to my habit of doing my best to think like my suspects. I didn't try to determine what I would do in their situations. More importantly, I tried to determine what *they* would do in their situations. There's a distinct difference, and as the following stories demonstrate, not everyone thinks this way. I didn't always think this way either, but the more I managed to do so, the more successful I became at doing my job humanely and well.

Educating the Victim

The direction in which education starts a man
will determine his future in life.

PLATO

Cold thefts and burglaries are probably the least exciting police work that can be done, but I hated suspending cases, so I put a lot of effort into solving them. This meant taking on a variety of monotonous tasks, since you never know which one will link you to another case or help determine who your suspect is.

Combining and linking cases to determine the specific habits of a criminal can solve many cases, and this team effort includes the victim. If you educate your victims, they will preserve the scene for you and assist you in locating stolen property. Sometimes, they even help you locate a suspect.

I was dispatched to a cold burglary at a military support maintenance shop. When I arrived on scene, the commanding officer told me that someone had broken into the facility, cut multiple locks, and stolen a large number of tools and equipment from one of the units.

I went to the southwest corner of the facility and saw where the chain link fence had been cut and pinned back. At this same location, it looked like a vehicle had become stuck. Inside the facility on the concrete was a camouflaged military Humvee. It was parked in an improper location and had been used to pull the suspect's vehicle from the ditch. This Humvee did not have a key to start; it just had an ignition lever and was padlocked with a cable that had been cut with bolt cutters.

I requested the on-call field evidence technician to help process the scene.

Multiple locks had been cut on the interior and exterior of the shed and identifiable suspect tire impressions were visible around the shed and secondary gate. Many tools had been stolen, but we had 100% accountability for all weapons and vehicles from the base.

The stolen items were unique; each had specific part numbers issued only to the military. I received photographs and a tool list so extensive, it took a full 96 pages. These hundreds of individual items needed to be entered one by one and had a total value of $75,000.

Our current academy class divided up the list and completed it in a few hours. This was a huge help for me, as it would have taken me quite a while to complete this on my own.

I collected and booked all the cut locks and chain links I could locate. I took overall pictures of the scene and close-up pictures of tire and shoe impressions. I processed the interior of the Humvee with DNA swabs on the ignition switch and steering wheel, and I put these into evidence with a water control so the swabs could be tested to determine that they hadn't been contaminated.

It appeared the suspect had cut the far western gate to leave the property after an unsuccessful attempt to exit through the primary electronic gate. I conducted an area check with the businesses directly to the south, all of which were vacant, and spoke with an employee at a business just north of the scene. I viewed the camera footage of the south lot that overlooked the scene and narrowed my time frame by an hour. Another employee had witnessed a Humvee with its lights on after 9:00 p.m., further narrowing the time frame.

I spent a lot of time talking to and educating the commanding officer and his personnel. I explained how they could install game cameras to help with any future investigations and also how they could aid in this investigation. I told them that after entering the tools as stolen, we would receive an alert if the tools were sold at a pawn shop, but I also explained that most thieves were now selling on local internet sites or taking tools to flea markets.

I explained that my sheriff's office and indeed most law enforcement agencies didn't possess the manpower to look online and at flea markets, and the commanding officer told me he'd assign personnel to assume these time-consuming tasks.

The fact is, no one is more motivated than the victim to solve the crime. What's more, any time victims can help, the feelings of helplessness and outrage they commonly feel somewhat dissipate.

In this particular case, I was aware of the military's motivation to catch the individuals involved, so I took extra time to explain how they could help us. If I hadn't taken this time, there's a very good chance we wouldn't have discovered the perpetrators, much less solved the other three related cases at military bases spanning several years.

Three days later, the base was burglarized again.

I arrived on scene and checked the perimeter of the property but didn't see any signs of vehicles or other disturbances. I got out of my vehicle, checked the chain and lock on the westernmost gate, and discovered the chain itself had been cut with what looked like bolt cutters.

Another deputy arrived on scene, and we continued to search for signs of the suspect. I advised dispatch to have the reporting party remain at the front of the property. On the interior of the base, a second gate had been cut. This time the suspect had cut the lock itself but not the chain.

Two of the mobile maintenance sheds were open with their locks cut. Tire impressions went between and around the vehicles to each side. The base commander called in personnel to do a complete inventory check of all weapons and vehicles to ensure there was no safety threat to the public. Once again, all vehicles and weapons were accounted for.

The other deputy and I processed the scene, taking photographs, swabbing for DNA, dusting for prints, and booking everything into evidence. The stolen property was now valued at $150,000.

A few days later, one of the military personnel spotted some of the missing tools being sold on an internet site. This lead developed a suspect, and this information was passed onto the strike team, a handful of patrol deputies who are assigned to do surveillance and to track individuals.

In this case, they pulled the individual over when he was leaving his residence to sell some of the tools. Some of the specialty tools were in plain sight, which allowed the strike team to write a search warrant for his residence.

I assisted in executing the warrant, and during the execution, I began giving clearance the serial numbers of equipment found on the scene. Several welders were flagged as stolen; these were linked to two other crimes at other military bases.

We then had military personnel check for other similar unsolved crimes in the region. Sure enough, another unsolved crime was linked to the case by the tire impressions left on scene that matched our suspect's vehicle.

In the end, educating the military as to how they could help solve the case was key. With their cooperation, we recovered a lot of tools and equipment and ended up solving five separate cases. These individuals were very detail oriented and enthusiastic about helping to catch the suspects, and it was a pleasure working with them.

Thinking about Their Kids

The future influences the present just as much as the past.

FRIEDRICH NIETZCHE

Most people care about their kids and care what their kids think of them. They don't want to traumatize their children or be seen in a negative light in front of them.

I always kept this in mind and did everything possible not to arrest people in front of their children. This took time and patience, but it gained me more respect and cooperation in the end and was simply the right thing to do. I never wanted children to see one or both parents being taken away in handcuffs.

One time, I was called to a residence by a woman who was concerned that her grown daughter was drinking and driving with her children, the woman's grandchildren, in the car.

The daughter had an active warrant, a revoked driver's license related to alcohol, and four additional active restraints, meaning she'd been contacted four times after having her license revoked.

When I arrived at the daughter's residence, I spoke with the daughter, who admitted she'd driven the children to and from her mother's house. I explained that I was going to arrest her and that I could do it in front of her children or wait until they left with their grandmother.

She thanked me for thinking of her children. She gave custody to her mother, who drove over to collect the kids, and I waited for them to leave before taking custody of the woman, arresting her, and transporting her to jail.

I always explained the situation to the person I was going to arrest and gave them a choice. If they cooperated, we would go out to my vehicle and I would cuff and transport them out of view of their children. If they didn't cooperate, I would take custody of them in front of their children.

Of the more than 100 people I arrested, when safety wasn't a concern and I was able to give them a choice, every person I took into custody chose option one. Being given this choice made them more respectful towards me, and every one of them thanked me for handling the situation this way.

Law enforcement routinely deals with the same people again and again, and simply showing some concern for how their children viewed them paid off in future encounters, too. When I subsequently met up with these individuals, they were more honest and cooperative, and many of them told me they were glad I was the officer who had responded to the call.

The inevitable conclusion: investing extra time and patience in the first encounter makes subsequent encounters better.

Understanding the People We Serve

*Every situation gives you the opportunity
to make it better or worse.*

I choose to try to make it better.

DARRON SPENCER

Here is an example of how thinking like the suspect
allowed me to catch the suspects in a fraud/theft case.
Initially, the victim believed she had lost her credit card
at a gas station, but later she realized the credit card had
been used at that same gas station and elsewhere after
she'd become aware that it was missing.

I went to the gas station and spoke with the store
manager, who provided me with the receipts and photographs of the transactions of the stolen credit card. An
employee at the gas station recognized the vehicle in the
video that the suspect was seen getting into. The purple
1996 Chevy Cavalier with the oxidized hood and notice-
able dent belonged to a woman who also worked at the
gas station.

I went to the owner's last known residence in a nearby
town and saw a vehicle with these features. The vehicle
and in-state plate came back listing the woman as the
registered owner.

Eventually, with the help of video, we determined that she and a man had used the stolen credit card at multiple locations. She'd physically swiped the card 21 times, spending a total of $1,430.11 in two cities and three towns, all of which were located inside the county as well as at a Walmart outside the county.

She also committed conspiracy by allowing the male to use both her vehicle and the credit card to purchase a variety of items on his own.

A few days later, once we had the story straight, I drove past the suspect's residence with my field training officer (FTO) sitting next to me. The vehicle wasn't there. I looked over at my FTO and reminded him that the woman had young kids. He nodded, and I said, "I know where they are." He looked confused and asked how I knew that. I said, "Well, she has young kids, no job, little money, and it's nice out. They're at the park."

I drove to the park, and sure enough, the purple vehicle was sitting in the parking lot. The FTO stated, "No freaking way."

A small group of people was sitting at a picnic table, and I recognized both the woman and the man from the surveillance video. I requested a second to be in route with a routine response because I knew I'd be arresting both people. I got out of my car and started walking toward the table, and the woman immediately got up and began walking towards me.

We met in the middle between the picnic table and my car. I said hello, addressing her by name, and commented that it was a nice day. She agreed, and I asked how old her kids were. After she told me, I asked her to explain what had happened and she openly admitted to finding the credit card and taking it. She also admitted to using the credit card and giving it to the male.

I asked if there was someone who could watch her kids and pick up the car, and she said her brother could take her kids home and her mom could watch them. I said, "I am going to have to arrest you, but do you want to first go give your kids a hug and I'll wait until they leave to take custody of you?" She said, "Yes, thank you."

I walked back over to the FTO who was standing by the car and told him she'd admitted to everything. He said, "Then why didn't you arrest her?" I said, "She's talking to her kids first; they're going to go back to her mom's house with her brother and after they leave, I'll arrest her." The FTO contemplated this, and then nodded in approval.

I interviewed the male in the public park. He admitted to using the credit card that the women had given him and said he'd used her credit card. I asked him what the name on the card was, and he stated it had someone else's name on it. I ran him through clearance, and he came back with a valid arrest warrant as well.

The woman walked over after her kids left and thanked me again for allowing her to say goodbye to them and for not arresting her in front of them.

I arrested both parties and placed them in belly belts for their comfort, then charged them each with three felonies and one misdemeanor.

Part of law enforcement's frustration is that after doing everything in our power to catch people who have broken the law, they are often released very quickly. This is partly because of overcrowding in jails and partly because of the additional charges individuals often receive after contact.

Law enforcement is responsible to some extent for the overcrowding and for the additional charges being filed, but if we gain people's cooperation instead of forcing compliance, we seldom have to file additional charges. Furthermore, this cooperation can be rewarded through the DA's office by the offer of better plea deals. This lightens the load on both the courts and jails while keeping those who don't want to cooperate in custody longer.

A week later, I was in a different district with the same FTO when I was dispatched to a suspicious vehicle that had been left running with the driver's side door open for two and a half hours with tracks leading into a cornfield.

The vehicle was a 1999 Mercury Cougar packed fairly full with a bunch of bags. I requested dispatch to ask the police department where the vehicle was registered to contact the owner, and the owner called and gave consent to search the vehicle. She also told me the only person who should be driving the vehicle was her mom.

I contacted the mother, who stated that she'd been driving with a woman whose last name she didn't know. They had stopped at a gas station in a nearby city, and the woman had taken off in the car when the mother went in to pay for the gas. She couldn't give me a time frame and said it had happened this morning. I asked why she hadn't reported the vehicle stolen, and she said she'd felt sorry for the woman.

Other deputies arrived on scene and located the woman on the northeast corner of the cornfield. She was wearing only her bra and panties and was armed with a large knife. She stated that she'd just killed someone in the cornfield and that there were two other men out there with shotguns attempting to kill her.

I searched the vehicle and discovered .1 grams of a crystalline structure that was positive on a presumptive NIK test for methamphetamine along with two glass pipes. I also discovered a yellow spiral containing information on the woman such as her date of birth and her purple vehicle.

That's when I realized I knew who the woman was – a week earlier, I'd arrested her for felony fraud and theft charges and she'd been released on a personal recognizance bond.

We placed her on a medical hold and transported her to the hospital, and the mother admitted the yellow spiral was hers. When I questioned her about the information in the spiral on the other woman, she became defensive and again stated that she'd just met the woman.

In total, 28 law enforcement personnel responded to the scene, including a SWAT team. If two men with shotguns were in the field, we couldn't take any chance. Sharpshooters watched from the tops of oil tanks while we searched the cornfield on foot with canines, but no one was in the cornfield and no one had been killed. Later, the woman admitted to eating a large amount of meth the previous evening when she'd been pulled over. After she was released from the medical hold, she was arrested.

As for the FTO, he told me I should go play the lottery. Law enforcement officers just didn't contact the same individual two weeks in a row in two different districts with a SWAT team on scene; it just didn't happen.

Laughing, I replied, "Apparently it does to me."

Stopping the Growing Trend

You cannot escape the responsibility of tomorrow
by evading it today.

ABRAHAM LINCOLN

Across America, certain dangerous trends are growing, among them school shootings, acquiring guns unlawfully, and spiraling narcotic drug dependencies, particularly heroin.

Law enforcement agencies actively train their people to handle these situations, including active shooter scenarios. It's vital to be prepared to respond to school shootings, but I believe more can be done to prevent them. One reason a career in law enforcement is a thankless profession is that few people know how many situations we interrupt before they become violent. Most people only know about the situations we don't interrupt.

In the following case, the help of law-abiding citizens made a real difference, although how big a difference, we'll never know.

Guns and Schools Don't Mix

Yesterday is not ours to recover,
but tomorrow is ours to win or lose.

LYNDON B. JOHNSON

One memorable case I worked on involved two special needs high school students who played a "game" each day at lunch. The game consisted of talking about how they would carry out an active shooting at their school and consisted of weapons they would use, who they would target, the targeting sequence, and how they would get away afterwards.

One of the fathers called the police after learning that his 17-year-old son had received a 9mm Smith and Wesson handgun with magazines and ammunition from another 17-year old student who shared a common interest in guns.

The friend gave the man's son ammunition at school and then brought a 9mm handgun to school and gave it to the boy. All told, the boy received the gun and well over 100 rounds of ammunition.

The young man's parents had secured the evidence and locked it in their bedroom safe. I had clearance run the serial number on the firearm, and it came back clear of any record. The two special needs students could not produce written statements, so I interviewed them multiple times during the course of my investigation.

My first interview was with the boy who had been given the ammunition and gun at school. He was familiar with the theater shooting that had recently made headlines. When I asked about the shooter in this case, he told me the shooter wasn't smart because of how he'd carried out the shooting and because he'd gotten caught.

I asked the boy if he'd hurt somebody he thought deserved to be hurt. He said he wouldn't but his friend most likely would because he had an anger problem. Here's a sample of our interactions during our first interview:

Me: "What do you and your friend talk about at school?"

Boy: "Um, we do stuff to each other that we do for fun like see how much pain we can inflict on each other. Um, most of the things we talk about is just for fun."

Me: "What do you talk about?"

Boy: "We mostly talk about guns and videogames and how we would use them."

Me: "How you would use the guns?"

Boy: "Um hmm. In the videogame or in real life."

Me: "Tell me about that. How would you use the guns in real life?"

Boy: "Um, we would probably take a bunch to like a shooting range and just fire some rounds off."

Me: "How would your friend use them in real life?"

Boy: "Um, I don't know what he would do with them in real life. And though we kind of talk about it he, he has more reasons, I don't, he has more reasons, even though he doesn't want to talk about them with me."

Me: "Okay. On a scale of one to 100, how likely do you think it would be for him to go into a school and shoot somebody? One being the least, 100 the most."

Boy: "Um, 50."

Me: "And how about yourself?"

Boy: "A zero."

I went to the residence of the other boy and explained what was going on to his parents. The boy wasn't home at this time. I asked his parents if they had any firearms in the residence. They did not, but the woman said her father might. She called him, and he was missing a box of 38 special rounds along with a 9mm Smith and Wesson. Turns out, the boy had stolen the gun and some ammunition from his grandfather from an unlocked box in the basement. He'd stolen the rest of the ammunition from his uncle.

I asked the parents if I could search their son's room, and they agreed and assisted me. Including them in the search was the right thing to do. They were very cooperative and wanted to know the truth as much as I did.

During the search, I discovered a small black case the other boy had told me his friend carried the firearm to school in. The parents agreed to meet with me again the next day when their son was home so I could interview him about bringing the gun and ammunition to school. Here's a sample of my interview with their son:

Me: "Okay. Can you start from the beginning and tell me why you needed a gun and whose gun it was? I've already talked to your friend, so I just need to know your side of the story."

Boy: "Uh huh, um, he, well, me and him like to talk about the Army and stuff, and he brought up, uh, he, uh, well, we always talk about guns and stuff."

Me: "Okay. Can you tell me why you gave him the gun?"

Boy: "Um, because we...I brought it up and he wanted it. I don't know."

Me: "You can be honest with me. That's why I'm here."

Boy: "Right. I don't know why he wanted it, but..."

Me: "Did he say he was going to do anything for you?"

Boy: "No." The boy squirmed in his seat, clearly uncomfortable with this question.

Me: "Did you talk to him about the gun, like he could have it, or how did the interaction between the two of you go?" The boy was mumbling a lot and avoiding an answer, so I changed the angle of my question. "What made you want to do this favor for him?"

Boy: "Um..."

Me: "'Cause it's a pretty good favor."

Boy: "Yeah. Well, it was, we were just like talkin' about guns and stuff, and I brought it up that I know somebody who owns guns and stuff."

Me: "Your friend said there's a lot of people who make you upset at school. He says you're pretty good about handling it so you don't act out against them. I was just trying to understand that a little better."

Boy: "I guess, um, there are some people that kind of make me, make me angry sometimes."

Me: "It's not okay that they make you angry. It's okay for you to be angry. Does that make sense?"

Boy: "Yeah."

Me: "Do you ever want to act on that anger?"

Boy: "Uh."

Me: "Do you understand you're not supposed to take guns to school?"

Boy: "Yeah."

Me: "Okay. Why did you choose to meet your friend at school to give him a gun versus somewhere else?"

Boy: "Um, 'cause I only see him at school. I don't see him outside of school."

Me: "Okay. And you like the guns?"

Boy: "Yeah."

Me: "What's your favorite gun?" Up to this point, I had been trying to drag information out of him. Now I wanted to determine his knowledge and proficiency of firearms.

Boy: "Um, um."

Me: "You okay?"

Boy: "Yeah. I would say the 50 caliber."

Me: "Yeah, okay. Have you ever shot a gun?"

Boy: "Uh, I shot a fake one, but not the, the heavy, heavy."

Me: "Do you know if your friend has shot guns?"

Boy: "No, I think, maybe. I don't really know."

Me: "Would you like to shoot guns?"

Boy: "Uh, uh, huh-huh. I was thinking about it, but, yeah."

Me: "You would?"

Boy: "Yeah. Just for hunting and stuff."

Me: "Have you ever thought about shooting anybody?"

Boy: "Um, no."

Me: "Okay. Why would your friend give me the impression that you've talked about shooting people?"

Boy: "Um, I don't know."

Me: "If you were the theater shooter, how would you have done it differently?"

Boy: "Uh, um, probably going to one of the rooms and then do it and then just go through and shoot everyone."

Me: "So you think he should've continued shooting people in the theater?"

Boy: "He should have gone in and sat down and then just shoot it and then..." He demonstrated how he would shoot from a seated position.

I asked the student how he would carry out a shooting at his high school. I wanted to see how much thought he'd given it, and I also wanted to compare what he said with what the other boy had said to see how closely their plans matched. This would help me determine whether or not they'd actually planned it.

The boy described in detail how he would carry out a shooting at his school, from the timing of the shooting to the path he would take to whom he would target first and why. He talked about how many guns he would need and how much ammo. The guns he described using weren't available to him, but everything else was detailed and believable. He talked about where he would hide the guns in the school and how he would get away. I had him draw a map of the school to get a better illustration of his plan, and he indicated on the map where in the school he'd given his friend the gun. His answers to my questions were quick and coherent, which led me to believe he'd given this quite a bit of thought.

I then asked him how his friend would carry out the shooting. He stated that his friend would go about it differently and would use a more believable type gun, a shortened shotgun. This level of detail concerned me and made me suspect the boy who had received the gun had not been completely honest with me.

I returned to this boy's house and spoke with his parents. I updated them on the case and asked to search their son's room, which I hadn't yet done. I explained that I wanted to determine if the boys had spoken about killing kids at school and to what extent. The mother completed a consent to search the residence, and the father asked if he could try something before we started.

I agreed, so the father addressed his son very sternly about the ammunition that wasn't accounted for and told him he'd better produce it.

The boy went directly to his bedroom with his parents and produced ammunition from numerous locations. In addition to what the boy produced, I found five rounds of .38 special hollow points in his backpack. He seemed genuinely surprised that the rounds were in his backpack.

The total search recovered 14 X .22 hollow points, 5 X .38 special hollow points, 5 X 9mm dummy rounds, 3 X 9mm FMJ, 2 X .410 shotgun shells, 2 X .42 novelty bullets, 1 X .410 spent casing, and 1 X .45 auto spent casing. Of the known stolen ammunition, the following ammunition was unaccounted for: 1 X 9mm FMJ, 1 X .38 special FMJ, and 1 X .38 special hollow point.

I asked the boy if he gotten any ammunition from his father, and he repeatedly stated no, that he'd gotten it all from the other boy. The father checked his ammunition and guns. Everything was accounted for, and his ammunition was a different brand.

I asked for clarification as to why the boy's friend had said he would use a short shotgun. The boy finally admitted that he and the boy played the "game," but his version was inconsistent and not nearly as detailed as his friend's.

This version included shotguns, a .22, a .410 shotgun, and also other people, including the other boy's Army cousin and the cousin's friends. I asked the boy if he knew if they were real people or not. The boy said he didn't know. I asked if he knew their names, and he said no. I asked if he knew where they lived, and he stated that he didn't.

I contacted the on-duty commander and informed him that my case could now possibly involve two more guns and two to three more people.

Turns out, the boy who brought the handgun to school had stolen it from his grandfather, who had noticed it missing two or three weeks earlier. I asked the grandfather why he hadn't reported the gun as stolen, and he stated that he thought he'd just misplaced it. The grandfather also stated that a week ago, he'd purchased a locking safe for the guns and ammunition and all of them were currently secure.

I asked the boy who received the gun if he'd participate if the game were real. He said no, that it would be wrong. I asked what he'd do if his friend were going to make the game real, and he said he'd immediately tell a teacher, counselor, or the SRO.

Nothing turned up in a coordinated search of the high school.

A detective and I returned to the home of the boy who had stolen the gun. The detective spoke with the boy and determined that the .410 ammunition and the .22 ammunition had come from his uncle's residence.

I contacted the uncle by phone, who physically checked to be sure he was still in possession of his .410 and his .22.

The parents of the boy informed us that the boy didn't have any cousins in the army.

At the end of the interview, I held up a .410 bullet and asked the boy what he planned to do with it. He told me he was going to make it part of the game. I said, "This bullet is real. How do you make it part of the game?" The boy remained silent but glared at me.

Neither of the boys was sent to the juvenile detention facility for several reasons, which I ultimately agreed with. Both were placed in the custody of their parents, put on home arrest, and suspended from school. Both were charged with minor in possession of a handgun and unlawful possession of a weapon on school grounds.

I'm fairly certain the boy who received the handgun had no intention of using it on people. I can't speak for the intentions of the boy who stole the handgun; you can draw your own conclusions. I learned the extent of their "game" by involving both sets of parents in the investigation. All four adults were beneficial to my investigation and critical to my success.

In law enforcement, you don't how much impact you've had because you can't know all the possible horrors you've prevented. By contrast, the ones we don't prevent are glaringly obvious.

Bad Guys Don't Get Background Checks

An investment in knowledge pays the best interest.
BENJAMIN FRANKLIN

Not surprisingly, bad guys don't get background checks before acquiring firearms. Here is a case that provides some insight on how they do get their firearms.

I was dispatched to a call about shots being fired on the county line. When I arrived on scene, I spoke with a police officer from the adjacent jurisdiction.

The officer stated he'd received a call about shots being fired from boats on a reservoir. When he'd arrived on scene, he'd observed a man firing an assault rifle from the hip.

I approached and spoke to the suspect, who stated that he was firing different assault rifles, two AKs and one AR, as well as a Ruger revolver.

I had the weapons cleared through dispatch and they all came back clear, which meant they'd never been reported as having been stolen or were known to have been used in a crime.

The suspect stated that he'd been firing at a satellite dish on the ground to the northwest, in a direct line of the reservoir.

I asked where the required raised backstop was so that he could shoot safely, and he indicated that the rise in elevation close to a half mile away was his backstop. This raised elevation was very short, only about three feet high.

I photographed all the firearms and their serial numbers. I noticed that on the Egyptian AK, the serial number was in a different location than on the other AK. The serial number was also not stamped but hand engraved. Its original location had obviously been modified and painted. This was interesting, since most guns are defaced because they've been stolen or used in a crime.

I asked the man where he'd gotten the firearm, and he told me he'd purchased it from a website a little over two years ago. This put the purchase just outside the time frame of new gun laws about buying and selling firearms.

I asked who he'd bought it from, and he couldn't remember. He thought he'd paid around $800.00 for it and said he wasn't aware it had been defaced. To be considered a crime, a person has to knowingly possess a defaced firearm.

I seized the Egyptian AK because it was obviously modified and defaced and explained that he couldn't sell or get rid of any of the firearms until this case was closed.

While I was photographing the firearms, I complimented the man on his choice in weapons to show my common interest in firearms. This got him talking. Whenever there was a pause in the conversation, he took the opportunity to tell me something new, including the fact that he'd just sold a lot of firearms.

I noticed a Hell's Angel support sticker in the back window of his truck. I asked if I could look in his truck, and he said yes. There was nothing criminal in the cab of the truck. I found an empty pistol holster behind the driver's seat. In the bed of the truck was a camouflaged ammo bag. He opened it to reveal different caliber magazines and miscellaneous ammunition. Among the magazines were SKS magazines for guns that were not on scene.

Instead of arresting him, I cited the man with reckless endangerment so that the gang task force could watch his movements and determine who he was working with. I was very pleased to have gotten my suspect to help me without him even knowing it. If people can relate to you and feel you share a common interest, they are usually more than happy to talk.

I had to stop working shortly after citing this man due to my medical condition, but it's very likely this guy was an arms dealer for the Hell's Angels biker gang. Accordingly, I forwarded the case to the Bureau of Alcohol, Tobacco, and Firearms so they could track the guns and the path they'd taken before ending up with him.

Krocodil, What's That?

No one is so brave that he is not disturbed
by something unexpected.

JULIUS CAESAR

This call scared me. I had no idea what I was witnessing or what I'd been exposed to, but that didn't stop me from trying to make the best of the situation.

I first became aware of the suspect when a woman came into the station to report a theft. The suspect had stolen fitness equipment from her and then pawned it. During the investigation, the suspect gave false information to pawnbrokers, and I also discovered he was suspended on an out-of-state license.

Three days later, the victim called and told me the suspect was driving her mother's vehicle. I located the vehicle and attempted to pull them over, but they drove several more blocks before pulling into the driveway at the mother's house.

The suspect got out of the driver's side door while an elderly woman got out of the front passenger door. She asked me to turn off my overhead lights, and I told her I would do so soon. When I asked the suspect for his ID, he produced an in-state ID card.

I had clearance run him, and he came back as suspended out of state. I spoke to him in a laidback manner and was not accusatory or judgmental in my questions or tone. I read him his Miranda rights and asked if he understood them, and he said he did. I asked if he wanted to continue to speak with me about the case, and he said he did. He admitted to stealing the equipment and pawning it and giving false information to the pawnbroker.

The suspect was sitting on the back of the forerunner with the rear door open, and I asked him to stand up. When he rose, I informed him that I was going to arrest him. I noticed a yellow residue on his left hand, so I told him not to move while I retrieved swabs and water to collect the evidence. During that time, I turned my overhead lights off to follow through on the elderly lady's request.

I collected the evidence and placed it in my car, then escorted the suspect to my vehicle with my bare hands on the back of his arm. He was wearing a black long-sleeved shirt, and it felt stiff, as though it had too much starch in it. I placed him in a belly belt for his comfort, reminded him of his Miranda rights, and asked when he'd last used heroine. He told me he'd used last night. I asked if the yellow stuff on his hand was heroine, and he said it most likely was.

I told him I was going to search him and asked if there was anything on his person that might hurt, poke, or stick me. He said he had two syringes in his right front pocket, so I put on protective gloves and began searching.

I removed two capped syringes from his front right pocket, pulled a grey bag out of his front left pocket with a similar color stain as his left hand, and bagged and secured the evidence in my trunk.

Next, I requested a K9 unit, but none were available. The elderly woman allowed me to search her vehicle and completed a consent to search form. I believe she allowed this because I'd turned off my overhead lights. I requested a second unit to assist with the search.

The woman asked if she could speak with the suspect while I was searching the vehicle. I told her she could not approach my vehicle while I was searching hers, but I did allow her to stand 15 feet away from the car and talk to him once I completed my search.

Depending on the type of case, and as long I know nothing can be passed or exchanged, I allow third parties to speak to the person I have in custody. More often than not, I overhear important information related to the case.

The interior of the forerunner was messy, with what appeared to be blood and puss on the doors, seats, and center console. My search uncovered a capped syringe, drug paraphernalia, and a handheld burner. The suspect told me he used the handheld burner to cook the heroin.

I secured all the evidence in the trunk of my patrol vehicle and transported the suspect to the jail. While he was in the booking vestibule, a nurse checked him out and said he needed to be cleared by the hospital. The suspect's long-sleeved shirt had been stuck to both of his arms, and when the nurse had peeled the sleeve off, she'd uncovered holes in his arms that went down to the membrane on his bones. It looked like his arms were rotting off. We were all quite nervous because we had no idea what had caused this. We feared it might be some terrible infection or flesh-eating bacteria.

I thought about the possibility of contagion and contamination. I was wearing a long-sleeved shirt, and I wondered if anything had touched my exposed skin. I had the booking officer watch the suspect while I went into the bathroom and vigorously washed my hands and arms with soap and hot water. I put on new gloves, placed the suspect in the back passenger side of my patrol car, and drove him to the hospital.

When the doctors came in, they were taken back by the gruesomeness of his arms. Due to the severity of his condition, I was instructed to leave him in the care of the hospital. In fact, I was told by my commander to unarrest him. The jail didn't want him in the facility because we didn't know what his problem was, nor did we want to be liable for paying his medical bill.

I drove back to the jail and had my patrol car decontaminated. At the end of my shift, I took everything off at the station and took a very long shower before changing into fresh clothes my wife brought me.

The next morning, the man went into surgery. Afterwards, the doctors stated that if he hadn't been brought in, they would have had to amputate both arms. They determined that the man's skin was rotting due to the type of heroin he was injecting, a product called krocodil, also known as the zombie drug, because its users eventually look like zombies.

I informed the drug task force of my suspect and his unique condition. To say the least, they were interested. This was the first confirmed case of krocodil in the state.

Several months later, the man was no longer working with the drug task force and I was allowed to contact him for some active warrants. My search uncovered three used syringes and two pill caps. I swabbed the inside of one of the pill caps and got a presumptive positive for heroine.

Once again, I took him to the hospital, and this time I received a medical clearance for him to remain in custody. His condition wasn't as bad as it had been previously. It also helped that the doctors knew what was causing his condition.

Since I had a good rapport with him, I asked where on his person he normally kept the heroin. He told me he kept it in his mouth in small baggies so he could swallow it if he were apprehended.

I know that progress was made in locating the dealer of the heroin, but the case was outside my jurisdiction, so I was never informed of arrests made or drugs seized.

The reason the suspect was so cooperative was that I showed him respect and never treated him poorly. In return, he assisted the drug task force and educated me on the specifics of how and why drug addicts go about transporting the drugs. Since I treated him like a normal human being and let him know I cared, he openly answered my questions. He was also thankful he hadn't lost his arms.

The point is, we can improve life for everyone if we treat people – suspects as well as everyone else – with the respect and dignity we'd like to be afforded.

CONCLUSION
Confronting the Abyss

If you gaze long enough into an abyss,
the abyss will gaze back into you.

FRIEDRICH NIETZCHE

As an officer of the law, I never woke up on any given day with the premonition that my life was about to change. Nonetheless, looking back, one case had special significance pertaining to my condition. Up until this point, I was sleeping more than usual but not feeling rested. I sensed that I wasn't as sharp as usual, but I chalked it up to being tired.

A serious red flag went up when, for the first time ever, I forgot to put my equipment in my duty belt, including my pistol, ammo, and taser. While this occasionally happens to law enforcement officers, they usually realize it right away and go and get whatever they forgot.

On this day, I attached myself to a domestic violence call, drove 30 minutes, and made an arrest, all without my equipment. I only noticed it was missing when I went to secure it in order to enter the jail.

This dangerous lapse scared the hell out of me, but I was too stubborn to admit that something was wrong. I just told myself I was tired. From that day on, I wrote myself notes and reminders of what I needed to do or take with me, constantly double and triple checking so that I wouldn't forget something. This continued for another three months, until I was physically unable to perform my job.

My medical condition is complicated. The doctors believe I have a slow spinal fluid leak, possibly due to a bone spur on the inside of a vertebra. This condition has affected almost every aspect of my life. I'm in the process of consulting with a neurosurgeon in California about the possibility of surgery on my spine. In another few weeks, my condition could be completely different or exactly the same.

On a good day, I wake up with my energy level around 65% and a constant pressure headache at the base of my skull. On a bad day, I wake up with my energy level around 40% and a headache so intense the left side of my face and neck goes numb, making it difficult to talk or swallow. The first time this happened, we thought I was having a stroke, but the doctors said I was having an atypical migraine with an aura that just happened to mirror a stroke.

Naturally, I've gone through different phases of coping. My initial reaction was to power through it and tackle the challenge head on. I kept working longer than I should have, and my condition progressed because I didn't listen to my body. I lost the ability to get restorative sleep, and that compounded my condition with double vision and a loss of cognitive function. Sleep deprivation is very harsh on the body, which is why it's utilized in torture.

After failing miserably to overcome this situation, I became very angry with myself. This anger carried over to my friends and family, though it wasn't directed at them. When I became aware of the impact I was having on my loved ones, I isolated myself. During this time, days seemed like weeks and weeks seemed like years. I felt like an inmate in solitary confinement.

Back when I was in boot camp, I went into what I call survival mode, honing my ability to get by on a meal-to-meal, day-by-day basis. I knew that my superiors couldn't stop time, and that meant I'd only be in these current harsh conditions temporarily.

The problem with a medical condition is that you don't have the luxury of knowing when it will end. There is no light at the end of the tunnel. If you know someone is going through something difficult, the standard reaction is to offer sympathy and ask about the individual's condition. I can only speak for myself, but one reason I stopped talking to people was that I didn't want to be treated like I was sick. I also hated trying to explain a condition that even my doctors didn't understand.

Thus, a word of advice: if you want to help someone in a tough situation, don't pity them. Instead, help them form new interests and memories. Don't remind them of their condition; distract them from it. Help them live instead of just survive.

Eventually, I quit trying to tackle the problem and began learning how to manage my symptoms. I learned the triggers for my condition and also my limitations, and I adjusted my life to accommodate those limitations. This was frustrating, but it led to small breakthroughs. Soon, I was successfully completing simple chores around the house, which gave me a sense of accomplishment and belonging.

The biggest breakthrough I made was to stop thinking about what I couldn't do and begin focusing on what I could do. This drastically affected my mood and is why I decided to write *Humane Policing*. While the task is bittersweet because I still can't actively pursue my passion for law enforcement, it does allow me to help others in a new way, one I never would have considered had I remained healthy.

For now, I'm focusing on the positive aspects of life. Right now, my number one goal is to get healthy enough for my six-year-old to tackle me. Probably 80% of my time is spent in bed, so my parents helped me build a desk that I can push over the bed so I can work.

For the past two years, I've had countless hours to analyze and reflect on how I did my job. I don't know if I'll ever be able to return to the physical rigors of law enforcement, but I'm cautiously optimistic.

In the meantime, I know I can help teach my brothers and sisters what worked for me and why. That's why I wrote *Humane Policing*, and it's why I started a business with the same name. My passion is to improve the world we live in, and I'm game to do it any way I can.

ABOUT THE AUTHOR

We are all in the gutter,
but some of us are looking at the stars.

Oscar Wilde

I am 39 years old, married, and have a six-year-old son. Raised outside a small town in southeast Texas, I played football and ran track and cross country in high school. After graduation, I joined the United States Marine Corps.

In the Marines, my primary job was infantryman with a secondary job of riot control. I was selected to the Marine Barracks at 8th & I St. in Washington, D.C., where I received special training in riot control. I was also trained in most of the ceremonial duties affiliated with funerals, the marching platoon, three round honors, cordons, appointments, retirements, inaugurations, the Tomb of the Unknown Soldier, Iwo Jima parades, Friday night parades at the barracks, and special assignments.

I will always remember participating in the cordon for Secretary of Commerce Ron Brown and the 34 others who perished in the 1996 plane crash in Croatia. The weather was grey and overcast with a heavy drizzle, which matched the mood that somber day.

Other special assignments included being positioned next to President Bill Clinton at a UN banquet at the Waldorf Astoria in New York City, attending events on the White House lawn, and escorting President Clinton's friends to an event. I was awarded the Meritorious Unit Commendation (Second Award), the Good Conduct Medal, the National Defense Service Medal, and received three letters of appreciation. I also possessed a Top Secret Department of Defense security clearance. My final rank was corporal (E-4).

I was then contracted to the Department of State, where I possessed a Top Secret security clearance and was assigned to the diplomatic mail and pouch facility and to the Turkish embassy. On one memorable occasion, I was assigned to a security detail for Yasser Arafat at his hotel in Washington, D.C.

While completing my associate's degree at Northern Virginia Community College, I organized and ran a semi-professional paintball team with a 20-person roster. We competed in 13 states over two and a half years. During this time, I became familiar with financing and sponsorships for non-mainstream sports teams and secured two regional sponsors with six local sponsorships for my team. Three national sponsors were interested until I broke my ankle. That ended my paintball career, and the team dissolved.

I then moved to Colorado to attend college at Colorado University in Boulder. My major was molecular, cellular, and developmental biology. Initially, I wanted to become a field researcher of level four viruses, but after a couple of years, I began questioning whether I wanted to spend approximately 20 years in school. I came to the conclusion that I did not, and after changing schools, I became certified as a peace officer, receiving my Peace Officers Standards and Training (POST) certification in 2004.

I was offered a position with a police department that was to begin six months after my interview. In the interim, I began helping a friend with his specialty construction business. When the police department's budget fell through and the department wasn't able to hire additional officers as planned, I started my own specialty construction and repair business. At its peak, I had 13 employees spread across three crews. The company was growing steadily when the economy crashed. I downsized as quickly as I could, but I was never able to fully recover and eventually was forced to file for bankruptcy. This experience completely altered my perspective. I went from $5,000.00 not being much money to $50.00 being a lot of money. All told, this helped me relate to others and prevented me from judging people based on their financial status.

Meanwhile, I was training with professional and college ice hockey players and attending professional scouting camps on the East Coast. Invited to attend a selection camp, I outplayed guys 10 years younger than me. The coach was impressed with my level of play, but he was concerned about my ability to maintain it and stay healthy given my age. This experience did answer my question regarding whether I was good enough to compete at a professional level.

After much consideration, I decided to pursue a career in law enforcement. I wanted a fulfilling profession that allowed me to help others, and after a short time, I knew I'd made the right choice. I went from a corrections officer to a sheriff's deputy and was in the patrol division for 20 months. During that time, I was responsible for 40 felony arrests and 74 misdemeanor arrests. I wrote 57 arrest affidavits, seven warrants for arrest, two production of records, and a single search warrant. I also assisted with four death investigations and booked over 150 items of evidence. I did the vast majority of my field evidence technician work and investigated almost all my own cases. I was also awarded Deputy of the Year and the Ribbon of Merit.

My career was my passion, but it came to an abrupt halt when I became disabled and unable to perform my duties. Forced to find a new way to help others, I decided to teach my unique approach and techniques to my brothers and sisters in law enforcement with the goal of bridging the gap between the general public and law enforcement while making our communities safer, happier places to reside.

For more information on how my approach can assist your agency and law enforcement personnel, visit www. Humanepolicing.com.

TESTIMONIALS

It was my pleasure not only to hire Darron but also to work with him. During his 20 months under my supervision, I was thoroughly impressed with his style and approach to law enforcement. He treated everyone humanely, with respect and fairness, and his approach led to unprecedented cooperation from career criminals. This resulted in more than 40 felony arrests and the filing of numerous misdemeanor charges.

Darron is now reaching out to agencies around the country to share his talents and unique style of law enforcement so that other officers and deputies can learn how he gains cooperation rather than forces compliance in order to solve major cases.

**— Senator John Cooke, Senate District 13,
former three-term sheriff of Weld County, Colorado**

It was a refreshing pleasure to work with Darron. As a detective, I could always count on him to be complete and thorough in his duties and tasks. He was eager to learn and willing to work hard. He often, if not always, went above and beyond expectations. He has a lot to offer law enforcement even as his promising career was cut short due to illness. He never forgot that we deal with humans, often at their worst, but still human beings. He treated people with warmth and friendliness. There is a time to be abrupt and take forceful command, verbal or physical, but this is unnecessary as a general rule. Most often, people responded well to Darron's style of policing. Using compassion, understanding, and empathy is beneficial in dealing with people, even suspects. If a police officer is angry and bitter in his dealings with people, he takes that poisonous attitude home to his personal life, too. It's fortunate that Darron is sharing his perspective. I hope law enforcement views it as the gift that it is.

—Terie Rinne Retired,
Weld County Sheriff's Office 33 Years